THE 2 AM CODE

THE EMPOWERMENT PLAYBOOK FOR CAREER AND PERSONAL SUCCESS.

LISA ANUGWOM NARH

FROM EXPERIENCE TO EMPOWERMENT: MY STORY AND PURPOSE

As I reflect on my experiences, I realize that I often made excuses or mentally minimized the unwanted advances I faced. I convinced myself that such situations were normal—telling myself, "This happens to everyone," or brushing it off as, "Men will be men." For a long time, I believed I had a superpower by simply deflecting these encounters. However, as I've grown and listened to the stories of women who have endured similar challenges, I see more clearly now: many women face these situations, not out of choice, but for survival or career progression. It's become evident to me that we need a guide—a roadmap—to navigate these experiences with confidence and empowerment.

This message is for women of all ages, including my own daughters, who are 10 and 12. It's important to me that they grow up with a clear understanding of what is acceptable behavior and what isn't. They should feel confident in saying "no" when necessary and in making decisions that honor their boundaries. It is my hope that they will speak out if they ever feel violated or pressured, fully aware that their self-worth is not tied to anyone else's expectations. My vision is for them to grow into empowered women, equipped with the tools to contribute positively to their relationships and professional environments.

I also hope that one day my daughters will read these pages and understand the experiences I've faced in becoming an advocate for women everywhere. This work is not only for those who have encountered these challenges but also for those who may not have—so they can recognize potential pitfalls and use the guidance here to prevent them. For women who have endured similar situations, I hope they realize they are not alone. The aim of this resource is to foster connection, create safe spaces for sharing stories, and validate the experiences we too often keep silent.

By writing this guide, my aim is to provide practical advice and emotional support to help women build self-efficacy, assertiveness, and resilience. I hope to inspire women to stand firm in their worth and create a more equitable and inclusive work environment. This resource stands as a testament to the strength and potential of women everywhere—a call to action for all of us to uplift, support, and inspire each other.

CONTENTS

INTRODUCTION

The phrase, "nothing good happens after 2 AM," along with the harmful sentiment that "the only thing open after 2 AM are your legs," has long perpetuated damaging stereotypes about women and their choices, especially in the workplace. *The 2 AM Code* aims to turn this narrative on its head, transforming what was once seen as a badge of compromise into a powerful manifesto for empowerment. This work is a declaration that no woman should have to sacrifice her dignity or comfort for her career. It's a rallying cry for all women: we can work, thrive, and stand firm against unwanted advances without losing our sense of self.

The reality faced by countless women across various professions—harassment, boundary violations, and the challenges of navigating spaces often shaped by gender power dynamics—cannot be ignored. The goal here is to equip you with the tools, strategies, and confidence to assert your boundaries, advocate for yourself, and handle these interactions with clarity and strength.

Within these pages, we will delve into the complex dynamics of power and gender in professional environments, breaking down the social norms that contribute to discomfort and harassment. Through shared experiences and practical advice, we'll uncover the invisible codes that influence behavior in these settings. You'll learn to recognize red flags, set effective boundaries, and respond to situations that challenge your autonomy.

You are not alone in this journey. By empowering yourself with knowledge and building a supportive community, you can rise above the challenges you face and reclaim your power, even in spaces that may feel hostile. This guide strikes a balance between practical strategies and empowering narratives, emphasizing that resistance can take many forms—whether it's speaking up for yourself or creating networks of support around you.

Together, we'll uncover strategies that will enable you to thrive in your profession without compromising your integrity. Whether you've personally experienced harassment or are determined to stand up against it, *The 2 AM Code* is your resource, your voice, and your pathway to a professional life where your skills, talents, and ambitions define you—not the inappropriate actions of others.

CHAPTER

01

MASTERING SELF-EFFICACY: THE FOUNDATION OF SELF-AWARENESS AND EMPOWERMENT

A Childhood Shadow

I was just a child, no older than five, when my sense of safety was shattered. It was a family friend's house, a place where laughter and play should have been the only things on my mind. We were a group of kids, playing under a blanket, when I felt it—a hand, unmistakably adult, creeping under the cover. It touched me in places that made me feel deeply uncomfortable. I looked up, confused and scared, but I couldn't fully grasp what was happening.

The feeling of violation was immediate and intense. I wanted to scream, to tell someone, but fear clamped my mouth shut. I felt like I would be in trouble if I spoke up. The memory of that hand haunted me, and I vowed never to return to that house.

Days later, as if to deepen my fear, the man appeared at our door. It was late, and I remember running into the bedroom, hiding under the bed, trembling with the fear that he would do it again. I stayed silent, too afraid to tell my parents or siblings. That night, and many nights after, I felt a profound sense of vulnerability and a desperate need to protect my body from unwanted touch.

That experience made me feel voiceless and powerless, but as I grew, I reclaimed my voice. Believing in my strength to overcome became the foundation of my empowerment—this is what self-efficacy is all about.

Understanding Self-Efficacy and Albert Bandura's Contributions

Self-efficacy, a concept developed by Albert Bandura, refers to an individual's belief in their ability to succeed in specific situations. Bandura's groundbreaking work demonstrated how this belief shapes how people think, feel, and act. Individuals with high self-efficacy see challenges as opportunities for growth, while those with lower self-efficacy may avoid difficulties, feeling overwhelmed by them (Bandura, 1997).

Bandura identified four key sources that influence self-efficacy: **mastery experiences**, where past successes reinforce confidence; **vicarious experiences**, where observing others' success inspires belief in one's own abilities; **verbal persuasion**, where positive feedback strengthens self-belief; and **emotional and physiological states**, where managing stress and emotions supports a confident outlook. These principles provide a powerful framework for building self-efficacy in the face of challenges (Bandura, 1997).

Bandura's principles of self-efficacy offer powerful tools for women to navigate the persistent challenges of gender bias and systemic barriers. By embracing small victories, seeking mentorship, and cultivating emotional well-being, women can build the resilience needed to overcome these obstacles and thrive. Strengthening self-efficacy is not just about individual growth—it's about rising above the limitations imposed by external forces, reclaiming the space to lead, and shaping a more equitable future.

_____

The 2 AM Code teaches us that mastering self-efficacy starts with asserting our right to exist on our terms. It's about knowing that you do not have to compromise your self-worth for anyone, at any time, especially in moments when the world seems to question your capabilities.

As we move from building confidence to exploring self-awareness, we uncover an essential truth: understanding ourselves at a deeper level is key to unlocking our full potential. Self-awareness enables us to channel our confidence with purpose, ensuring our actions align with who we are and what we stand for. Now, let's delve into the power of self-awareness and how it amplifies both our self-efficacy and professional success.

Practical Applications of Self-Efficacy and Mindfulness for Navigating Workplace Challenges

As women put self-efficacy into practice—whether in meetings, negotiations, or leadership roles—they naturally build confidence. But self-efficacy also deepens self-awareness, revealing the emotions, strengths, and areas for growth that shape their professional journey. Confidence, when grounded in self-awareness, becomes the key to navigating challenges with purpose and resilience.

Facing Gender Bias in Meetings: Remaining composed through breathing techniques allows women to assert their contributions confidently, even when their ideas are overlooked.

Navigating Cultural Differences: Bridging cultural gaps requires empathy and self-assurance, fostering mutual respect in diverse teams.

Pursuing Leadership in Male-Dominated Environments: Mentorship and small successes build leadership skills, while centering oneself helps reduce pre-interview anxiety.

Managing Workplace Conflict: Addressing conflict with clarity, rather than emotional reactions, ensures resolution and strengthens professional relationships.

Negotiating for Equal Pay: A clear understanding of your worth, backed by data, helps frame confident negotiations, while staying calm ensures a composed dialogue.

Addressing Microaggressions: Staying composed in the face of subtle discrimination allows for an assertive and constructive response that encourages professional growth.

Leading Inclusively: Leading with empathy and staying open to diverse perspectives builds trust and elevates team dynamics, creating a more inclusive environment.

Confidence, rooted in self-efficacy, drives women to take initiative, communicate assertively, and handle difficult situations with resilience. It's more than just belief in one's abilities—it's about how that belief shows up in everyday workplace interactions, empowering women to lead, collaborate, and face challenges with purpose.

With self-efficacy, women lead assertively, manage conflict with confidence, and navigate professional dynamics with resilience and purpose. Whether it's speaking up in meetings, negotiating fair compensation, or addressing conflict, this inner belief drives how effectively these moments are navigated. It empowers women to lead with quiet authority, build strong professional relationships, and remain composed under pressure.

While confidence is crucial, pairing it with self-awareness is what turns it into a transformative force. Understanding our emotions, strengths, and areas for growth allows us to align our confidence with intentional actions, ensuring long-term success.

Understanding Self-Awareness

Self-awareness is key to understanding how your emotions and actions affect others. While the concept has roots in ancient philosophy—Socrates' famous "Know thyself"—it gained formal recognition in modern psychology through the work of Shelley Duval and Robert Wicklund in 1972. They introduced the concept of objective self-awareness, a process where individuals evaluate their behavior against internal standards and values, leading to greater alignment between actions and personal goals (Duval & Wicklund, 1972).

This self-evaluation process is essential for personal growth, as it fosters a deeper understanding of one's strengths, weaknesses, and impact on others. By cultivating self-awareness, individuals can make more informed decisions, improve their relationships, and ultimately live in closer alignment with their values.

Self-awareness is the complement to self-efficacy in professional settings. By understanding their strengths, weaknesses, and emotional responses, women can confidently apply their self-efficacy in overcoming systemic barriers like gender bias and underrepresentation in leadership roles.

Building Self-Awareness in Professional Settings

Encouraging reflective practices such as journaling, mindfulness, and meditation is essential for enhancing self-awareness. These practices allow women to take a step back, assess their emotions, and gain deeper insight into their thoughts and behaviors. When combined with emotional intelligence, this self-awareness becomes a powerful tool for managing emotions and understanding how they affect others. By developing emotional intelligence, women can foster more effective communication, resolve conflicts with empathy, and lead with greater authenticity. These practices are not just about self-reflection but about building the emotional capacity to connect with others and navigate complex professional dynamics with confidence and composure.

Creating a culture of constructive feedback is another key to growth. Seeking feedback from colleagues, mentors, and supervisors allows women to gain multiple perspectives on their performance and leadership style. This feedback serves as a tool for continuous improvement, sharpening skills and reinforcing strengths. Embracing feedback as an opportunity for growth empowers women to become more adaptable and effective in their roles.

Understanding your strengths and weaknesses through self-assessment tools and reflection is essential for personal and professional growth. By recognizing your unique talents and areas for development, you can make informed decisions about your career path, capitalize on your strengths, and continue to evolve in alignment with your goals.

Mindfulness is the practice that allows us to stay grounded in the present moment, observing our thoughts and feelings without judgment. Incorporating mindfulness into daily routines empowers us to regulate emotions, reduce stress, and gain clarity, strengthening our resolve to face professional challenges with calm and purpose. This heightened awareness becomes a foundation for stronger self-efficacy, empowering us to not only understand our capabilities but to believe in them fully (Kabat-Zinn, 2012).

As we build self-awareness through mindfulness, we strengthen our ability to face challenges with resilience, stay composed in difficult situations, and maintain clarity when making decisions. This balance of awareness and action is the key to mastering self-efficacy, enabling us to navigate life's complexities with confidence and purpose.

Harnessing Mindfulness for Professional Success

Mindfulness empowers professionals to stay present, make intentional decisions, and maintain composure in high-pressure situations. Whether navigating difficult conversations or recovering from setbacks, it fosters resilience and emotional clarity, ensuring thoughtful responses in even the most challenging moments.

Practical Applications of Mindfulness in Professional Scenarios:

Decision-Making in High-Stress Meetings: During a tense meeting where quick decisions are required, mindfulness allows you to pause, center yourself, and make clear, intentional choices without reacting impulsively to pressure. This focus ensures that your decisions are aligned with long-term goals rather than immediate stress.

Recovering from Setbacks: When faced with a project failure or personal setback, practicing mindfulness helps you regulate your emotions and bounce back more quickly. By staying grounded, you can calmly assess the situation, adjust your approach, and move forward with renewed focus and determination.

Navigating Difficult Conversations: In challenging discussions with colleagues, mindfulness enables you to listen actively and respond with empathy rather than defensiveness. By being fully present, you can address issues constructively, fostering mutual understanding and stronger working relationships.

Building Collaborative Teams: As a leader, using mindfulness can help you stay attuned to the needs and emotions of your team members. This awareness allows you to create a more inclusive and supportive environment, where individuals feel heard and valued, ultimately enhancing team collaboration and performance.

As you've discovered, mastering self-efficacy and mindfulness is the cornerstone of personal and professional success. Now is the time to reflect on your strengths, seize the opportunities for growth, and fully embrace the power of self-efficacy. This guide will support you as you move toward even greater personal and professional fulfillment. The following assessment will help you measure your current position and set a clear course for your continued empowerment.

CHAPTER 1
ASSESSMENT: UNDERSTANDING SELF-EFFICACY AND SELF-AWARENESS

Assessment: General Self-Efficacy and Self-Reflection Scale

Instructions: Rate each statement on a scale from 1 (Strongly disagree) to 5 (Strongly agree).

1. I believe I can achieve my goals even when faced with obstacles.
2. I frequently reflect on my thoughts and feelings.
3. I am confident in my ability to handle unexpected situations.
4. I am aware of my strengths and weaknesses.
5. I can find solutions to most problems I encounter.
6. I feel capable of learning new skills.
7. I can stay calm under pressure.
8. I regularly set and achieve personal goals.
9. I am aware of how my emotions affect my actions.
10. I can adapt to changes and challenges effectively.

Scoring Interpretation

- 10-20: Low Self-Efficacy and Self-Awareness

   Description: Individuals in this range may struggle with confidence in their abilities and have limited awareness of their strengths and weaknesses. They might find it challenging to set and achieve goals, handle unexpected situations, and reflect on their thoughts and emotions.

Action Steps:

1. Set Small, Achievable Goals: Start with tasks that are easily manageable to build confidence.

2. Daily Self-Reflection: Keep a journal to reflect on daily experiences and emotions.

3. Seek Support: Surround yourself with supportive people who encourage and believe in you.

- 21-35: Moderate Self-Efficacy and Self-Awareness

Description: Individuals in this range have a moderate level of confidence and self-awareness. They can handle most situations but may still experience occasional self-doubt. They are somewhat aware of their strengths and weaknesses and engage in self-reflection.

Action Steps:

1. Challenge Yourself: Set slightly more challenging goals to push your limits.

2. Mindfulness Practices: Engage in mindfulness exercises to enhance self-awareness.

3. Seek Feedback: Ask for constructive feedback from peers or mentors to improve and grow.

- 36-50: High Self-Efficacy and Self-Awareness

Description: Individuals in this range are highly confident in their abilities and have a strong awareness of their strengths and weaknesses. They regularly set and achieve goals, handle unexpected situations with ease, and engage in deep self-reflection.

Action Steps:

1. Take on Leadership Roles: Volunteer for leadership positions or projects to further develop your skills.

2. Mentor Others: Share your knowledge and experience by mentoring others.

3. Reflect on Growth: Regularly reflect on your personal and professional growth to maintain and enhance your self-efficacy.

You've now completed your first step toward building a strong foundation of self-efficacy. Recognizing your internal strengths and embracing the belief that you are capable of achieving your goals is the cornerstone of your empowerment journey. But self-awareness is just the beginning.

Now, it's time to translate that self-belief into action by mastering assertiveness. Join me in **Chapter 2**, where you'll discover how the power of saying "no" can unlock even greater control over your professional and personal life.

02

THE ART OF ASSERTIVENESS: HARNESSING THE POWER OF SAYING NO

Chapter 2: The Power of Saying No with insights on empowerment, techniques for declining requests, and strategies for navigating pushback.

A Brother's Betrayal: Navigating Unwanted Advances from Those We Trust

In the fast-paced, high-stakes world of finance, trust is a currency as valuable as any stock or bond. I never imagined that betrayal would come from someone I considered family. My close friend, practically a brother, had been a constant presence in my life, both professionally and personally. We had shared countless late nights strategizing over market trends and celebrating our successes. His wife had just given birth to their fourth child, and I had been there to support them through the joyful milestones.

One day, he asked to speak with me privately. We sat in his car, a familiar setting where we had often discussed everything from business deals to personal dreams. But this time, the atmosphere was different—tense and charged with an unspoken weight. He turned to me, his expression serious, and said, "I've been thinking about this for a long time. I want to sleep with you."

The words hung in the air, heavy and shocking. I felt a wave of disbelief and nausea. This was a man I trusted implicitly, someone whose family I cared for deeply. His proposition was not only inappropriate but also deeply unsettling, given the recent birth of his child. The betrayal cut deep, and I struggled to find my voice.

Summoning my strength, I firmly told him this was unacceptable and left the car, my heart pounding. Moments later, he approached me again, desperation in his eyes, asking if I was sure it would never happen. His persistence was alarming, and I realized I needed to set a clear boundary. I threatened to tell his wife if he ever made another inappropriate advance.

The betrayal shattered my trust and left me feeling vulnerable and disillusioned. The professional environment I once thrived in now felt tainted, forcing me to confront the importance of setting boundaries and standing up for myself. It was a turning point that contributed significantly to my decision to leave the finance world behind.

This personal experience taught me that assertiveness is crucial not just for dealing with betrayals, but for navigating all aspects of life. Whether in personal relationships or the workplace, the ability to assert one's boundaries is fundamental to maintaining integrity and control.

Empowerment Through Refusal

This incident marked a pivotal moment in my journey toward assertiveness. It taught me that saying no, even in uncomfortable situations, is an act of self-preservation and empowerment. My experience is far from unique. In fact, many women face similar situations in their personal and professional lives, often feeling the weight of societal expectations to be accommodating, even when it compromises their well-being. This pressure to say 'yes' is ingrained early, shaping how we communicate in the workplace and making assertiveness a skill we must actively develop (O'Neill & O'Reilly, 2011).

Understanding Assertiveness and Its Power

Assertiveness allows individuals to express their thoughts and needs clearly while respecting others. It isn't just about refusing requests—it's about valuing your own limits. Historically, assertiveness became prominent during the human potential movement, with psychologists developing training programs to help individuals shift from passive or aggressive behaviors to more balanced, assertive communication (Salter, 1949).

The Assertiveness Paradox for Women

Women often face unique challenges when being assertive, with research showing they may be perceived as aggressive when they speak up. This "assertiveness paradox" creates a fine line for women who want to assert their needs without being penalized for it. Understanding these societal expectations allows women to navigate them more strategically (Rudman, 1998).

Historical Context of Assertiveness

The concept of assertiveness gained prominence in the mid-20th century as part of the human potential movement. Psychologists like Andrew Salter and Joseph Wolpe developed assertiveness training programs to help individuals overcome passive or aggressive communication styles. These early programs laid the groundwork for the techniques we use today, emphasizing practical strategies like role-playing and feedback. By practicing these methods, women can develop the skills needed to assert their boundaries in both personal and professional settings (Wolpe, 1958).

Assertiveness is a powerful tool for professional success and personal empowerment. By understanding the historical context and unique challenges women face in developing assertiveness, we can create strategies to support and encourage assertive communication in the workplace. As we continue to break down obstacles and promote gender equality, assertiveness will play a crucial role in empowering women to achieve their career goals.

The Empowerment of Saying No: Redefining Boundaries

Saying no is a powerful tool for protecting your time, energy, and integrity. It reinforces boundaries, signals self-respect, and helps build healthier relationships by eliminating power imbalances. By asserting yourself through the act of refusal, others are more likely to view you as someone who commands respect and is serious about their limits.

Moreover, saying no is an act of self-care, enabling you to prioritize your needs and well-being over external pressures that could compromise your comfort or integrity. Establishing boundaries through refusal not only promotes healthy relationships but also eliminates imbalances of power and dependency. Despite its importance, many struggle with saying no due to societal expectations and the fear of disappointing others. Historically, refusal has carried a negative connotation, but as early as childhood, saying "no" becomes a key assertion of autonomy. In the mid-20th century, psychologists began emphasizing assertiveness training as a way to reclaim this vital skill, highlighting its role in self-expression and self-care.

At the heart of The 2 AM Code is the principle that saying no is not only your right but your power. It teaches you to stand firm in your decisions without guilt, knowing that protecting your time and well-being is non-negotiable.

Emotional Intelligence and the Power of Saying No

Learning to say no is deeply connected to emotional intelligence (EQ), a key factor in maintaining healthy relationships, improving job performance, and cultivating leadership skills (Goleman, 1995). By utilizing emotional intelligence, individuals can recognize when to set boundaries and manage their emotions and interactions with others more effectively. Far from being a negative or selfish act, saying no is an instrument of self-respect and integrity. It prevents exploitation and allows individuals to focus on their own goals and values. Leaders who exercise the power of saying no with emotional intelligence demonstrate clear decision-making and foster respect within their teams, setting a standard of healthy boundaries and authentic leadership. In this way, saying no becomes not just an act of self-preservation but also a sign of strong leadership, reinforcing a culture of respect and balance.

Saying no is often misunderstood as a negative or selfish act. However, saying no is an act of emotional intelligence—it's about understanding your limits and valuing your time and energy. Leaders who exercise emotional intelligence when saying no demonstrate self-respect and set clear boundaries, which in turn builds respect within their teams.

Mastering the Art of Saying No

1. **Assertiveness Training Through Role-Playing**: Practical role-playing exercises can be immensely helpful in preparing for real-world scenarios where saying no is necessary. For instance, imagine a superior asks you to take on additional work when your plate is already full. In this case, a firm but respectful response might be, "I appreciate the trust you have in me, but with my current workload, I won't be able to give this project the attention it deserves. Could we discuss reprioritizing tasks or allocating this to another team member?" Practicing these situations in a training environment will build your confidence to handle similar requests in real life.

2. **Self-Reflection and Journaling**: Reflect on past situations where saying no was particularly challenging. For example, you may have found it difficult to refuse a request for after-hours work that disrupted your personal time. Journaling about these experiences helps you identify the emotional barriers that make saying no hard—perhaps the fear of disappointing others or losing favor at work. By understanding these patterns, you can mentally prepare for future situations and develop strategies to assert your boundaries without feeling guilt.

3. **Positive Framing in Real-Time**: A great way to assertively decline a request without feeling abrasive is to use positive framing. For instance, if a colleague asks you to take on an additional project that you don't have time for, you can say, "I appreciate you thinking of me for this, but I'm currently focused on another priority. I'd love to help at a later time when I can give it my full

attention." This approach maintains professionalism and offers a solution while firmly protecting your time.

4. **Support Networks for Guidance**: Mentorship and peer networks are invaluable when facing difficult decisions about setting boundaries. For example, if you're navigating an uncomfortable situation like inappropriate advances in the workplace, seeking advice from a trusted mentor can provide clarity and emotional support. Your mentor may guide you on how to handle the situation professionally, such as saying, "I value our working relationship, but this behavior is crossing a line. Please stop, or I'll need to escalate this." Having a support system helps you feel validated and empowered when asserting your boundaries.

The 2 AM Code demands we take control of our choices. Saying no is an act of leadership—it's a refusal to let others define your limits or compromise your boundaries.

While assertiveness techniques can be applied in most professional settings, it's important to recognize that communication styles vary significantly across cultures (Hofstede, 1980). In some places, direct refusals may be seen as assertive and confident, while in others, they might come across as rude or confrontational. For example, in the U.S., direct communication is often valued, and saying "no" clearly can be seen as a strength. However, in East Asian cultures, saying "no" too bluntly may be considered disrespectful. People may say "yes" out of respect even when they mean "no," or they might prefer to decline indirectly to maintain harmony. In Japan, for instance, a polite refusal might sound like, "That might be difficult," rather than a direct "no." Understanding these cultural nuances allows you to maintain professionalism while asserting your boundaries in a way that is respectful and appropriate, no matter where you are.

During my tenure as CFO of an organization, I was responsible for managing finances, payroll, and HR operations. Despite my diligent oversight, I noticed recurring financial discrepancies that puzzled me for months. Determined to uncover the truth, I conducted thorough research and discovered a shocking misuse of funds by the executive director. Instead of directly embezzling money, he purchased gift cards at grocery stores, which he then used for personal expenses, including cash withdrawals and luxury items.

Upon this revelation, I was filled with a mix of anger and resolve. I had only a few hours to decide my course of action. As the sole female member of an all-male management team, I knew I had to act decisively and assertively. I convened a meeting with the entire team and laid out the evidence of the executive director's misconduct. I presented a clear ultimatum: he could either hand over his credit card immediately, relinquishing any access to the organization's finances, or I would resign on the spot.

To my relief, he chose to give up all financial obligations, allowing us to move forward and restore integrity within the organization. Although I had no idea what the outcome would be that day, I knew it was my responsibility to do the right thing.

This experience was a profound test of my integrity and resilience. By standing firm and confronting the issue head-on, I demonstrated my commitment to ethical leadership and the well-being of the organization. It wasn't just about safeguarding finances; it was about upholding my self-worth and the principles I believed in. This moment underscored the undeniable power of saying no—of standing up for what's right, even when it's uncomfortable.

Mastering the power of saying no goes beyond setting boundaries—it's about leadership, integrity, and self-respect. Every time you say no to something that doesn't align with your values, you're saying yes to your goals, your future, and your well-being. It's time to act. Claim your space with confidence and let your refusal become your affirmation of who you are and where you want to go.

Next, the upcoming assessment will help you evaluate how assertive you are in various situations. By understanding your strengths and identifying areas for growth, you'll take a bold step toward mastering assertiveness in every facet of your life.

ASSESSMENT: ASSERTIVENESS SCALE

Instructions: Rate each statement on a scale from 1 (Never) to 5 (Always).

1. I feel comfortable saying no to requests that are unreasonable.
2. I can assert my needs without feeling guilty.
3. I stand up for myself in difficult situations.
4. I can decline invitations or offers without feeling pressured.
5. I communicate my boundaries clearly.
6. I can handle others' reactions when I say no.
7. I feel confident in my ability to refuse additional work when I am already busy.
8. I can say no without feeling the need to justify myself.
9. I respect my own limits and prioritize my well-being.
10. I can negotiate compromises when necessary.

Scoring Interpretation

- 10-20: Low Assertiveness

   Description: Individuals in this range may find it difficult to say no and assert their needs. They might feel guilty or pressured when declining requests and struggle to communicate their boundaries clearly.

Action Steps:

   1. Practice Saying No: Start by saying no in low-stakes situations.

   2. Use "I" Statements: Express your needs using "I" statements to communicate assertively.

   3. Set Clear Boundaries: Identify your personal boundaries and practice communicating them.

- 21-35: Moderate Assertiveness

Description: Individuals in this range are moderately assertive. They can say no and assert their needs in most situations but may still experience occasional discomfort or guilt. They communicate their boundaries but might struggle under pressure.

Action Steps:

1. Role-Play Scenarios: Practice assertive communication with a friend or mentor.

2. Reflect on Past Experiences: Think about past situations where you successfully asserted yourself and what you can learn from them.

3. Set Firm Boundaries: Reinforce your boundaries and practice maintaining them even under pressure.

- 36-50: High Assertiveness

Description: Individuals in this range are highly assertive. They feel confident saying no and asserting their needs without guilt. They communicate their boundaries clearly and handle others' reactions effectively.

Action Steps:

1. Continue Asserting Needs: Maintain your assertiveness in all situations.

2. Mentor Others: Help others develop their assertiveness skills.

3. Reflect on Successes: Regularly reflect on your assertive interactions and celebrate your successes.

Congratulations on embracing the art of assertiveness! Saying "no" is not a weakness but a form of empowerment that gives you control over your time, energy, and focus. By using assertiveness effectively, you've taken an essential step toward ensuring that your voice is heard and respected.

In the next chapter, we'll build on these skills by helping you **define and communicate your boundaries** in a way that solidifies your authority. Let's dive into **Chapter 3**, where you'll learn to protect your space and maintain the professional respect you deserve.

03

DEFINING YOUR SPACE: STRATEGIES FOR ESTABLISHING AND COMMUNICATING BOUNDARIES

"The Elevator Encounter: Standing Firm Against Unwanted Advances

The Elevator Incident

I was working as a personal assistant to a powerful figure in the organization. I respected him immensely and enjoyed my role, which involved managing his schedule, coordinating meetings, and ensuring everything ran smoothly. He was a charismatic leader, someone who commanded respect and admiration from everyone around him. I felt privileged to be in such a position, learning from one of the best in the industry.

One day, as we rode the elevator up to the office, the usual hum of the machinery seemed louder in the confined space. He leaned toward me, grabbing my belt buckle. Shocked, I pushed back and firmly said, 'Not going to happen.' The elevator ride was heavy with unspoken tension, but what I didn't fully grasp at the time was the importance of asserting my boundaries in that very moment. This experience, though unsettling, became the first in a series of lessons that underscored how essential it is to define and protect your space, both personally and professionally.

This incident, and others like it, highlight a critical truth: we need clear boundaries in both personal and professional spaces to maintain our integrity and well-being. Let's explore how to establish and communicate these boundaries effectively.

Establishing and Communicating Boundaries

In a world where the demands of work and personal relationships often blur the lines, establishing and communicating boundaries becomes crucial for maintaining mental health, productivity, and healthy relationships. This chapter delves into understanding, articulating, and upholding boundaries effectively (Cloud & Townsend, 1992)..

With 'The 2 AM Code,' you reclaim the power to define your space. Whether facing unwanted advances or overreaching demands at work, this code serves as a guide to protect your boundaries, without fear of backlash.

The Power of Boundaries

Boundaries allow us to define our space, protect our energy, and maintain control over our personal and professional lives. Establishing clear boundaries helps ensure that our interactions are respectful and productive. As Dr. Jordan Peterson aptly puts it, boundaries delineate our personal domain, helping us navigate life's complexities with clarity and purpose (Peterson, 1999).

Over time, the concept of boundaries has evolved. Historically, the workplace was seen as a public, male-dominated sphere, while home life was relegated to the private, feminine sphere. But as women entered the workforce and the lines between work and personal life blurred, boundary-setting became more essential than ever. The rise of the human potential movement in the mid-20th century brought renewed focus on boundaries, and psychologists developed strategies to help individuals manage their roles across multiple domains.

Key Boundary Management Strategies

With "The 2 AM Code" our space is ours to define, and no one has the right to cross those boundaries. Whether you choose to keep life domains separate or allow them to overlap, the power lies in deciding what works best for you.

There are multiple strategies for managing boundaries effectively, each catering to different personal needs and circumstances. **Segmentation** is where you keep work and personal life separate, ensuring tasks don't spill over from one domain to another (Ashforth, Kreiner, & Fugate, 2000). For instance, setting strict work hours or having a no-work policy during family time creates a clear divide. On the other hand, **integration** offers more fluid boundaries, where work and personal tasks might overlap—like responding to emails while attending family events. While this strategy provides flexibility, it also requires careful management to avoid burnout. **Role prioritization** helps you decide which life domain takes precedence in different situations, allowing you to maintain focus when multiple demands arise. The key to any of these methods is clear communication—letting others know when you are unavailable or prioritizing certain commitments ensures your boundaries are respected.

Once you've chosen your boundary strategy—whether it's segmentation or role prioritization—using these techniques can help you communicate your boundaries effectively and ensure they are respected.

Effective Techniques for Establishing and Communicating Boundaries

Establishing boundaries isn't a one-size-fits-all approach. Each of us must discover the strategies that best suit our lives. Let's explore different approaches to boundary-setting that can empower you to take control of your space.

1. **Self-Awareness**: Start by understanding your own needs and limits. Reflect on past experiences where your boundaries were

either respected or violated, and use those insights to define what's non-negotiable for you.

2. **Clear Communication**: Use assertive "I" statements to express your needs, like "I need time to focus on this project without interruptions."

3. **Consistency**: Once you establish boundaries, uphold them. Frequent exceptions may lead others to disregard your limits.

4. **Flexibility**: Be willing to adjust boundaries when necessary, but ensure these adjustments are the exception, not the norm.

5. **Support Systems**: Surround yourself with colleagues, mentors, and friends who respect your boundaries. They will reinforce your limits when challenges arise.

6. **Self-Care**: Prioritize your well-being to maintain resilience. Regular self-care routines—exercise, meditation, or hobbies—allow you to recharge and reinforce your boundaries.

Defining your space through the establishment and communication of boundaries is a powerful strategy for personal and professional empowerment. By understanding the historical context and unique challenges associated with boundary setting, particularly for professional women, we can develop effective strategies to protect our time, energy, and integrity. As we continue to promote gender equality and create more inclusive work environments, the ability to establish and communicate boundaries will be a crucial tool in empowering women to achieve their career goals (Markman, Stanley, & Blumberg, 1994).

Expressing Boundaries Professionally

In the workplace, boundaries need to be expressed clearly yet professionally (Goleman, 1995). Here's how to communicate effectively:

- **Use "I" Statements**: Frame your boundaries in a way that focuses on your needs, such as, "I feel overwhelmed when deadlines are moved without notice."

- **Be Direct and Honest**: Vague responses like "I'm busy" can lead to miscommunication. Instead, say, "I can commit to this next week, but I'm unavailable until then."

- **Nonverbal Communication**: Reinforce your message through body language—stand tall, make eye contact, and maintain a calm tone to show confidence.

- **Active Listening**: Show understanding of others' responses to your boundaries. This fosters mutual respect and opens space for dialogue.

Cultural Differences in Boundary Setting:

Setting boundaries is essential for safeguarding your personal space and mental well-being, but the way you communicate them can vary depending on cultural context. In some regions, direct communication is appreciated as clear and assertive, while in other areas, such as many West African or Latin American cultures, a more nuanced, indirect approach is often preferred to maintain relationships and show respect. For instance, instead of saying a firm 'no,' a phrase like 'I'll see what I can do' or 'Let me think about it' might be used to soften the refusal. Understanding these cultural differences allows you to navigate diverse work environments with professionalism, ensuring that your boundaries are respected while being sensitive to varying communication styles (Hofstede, 1980).

Techniques for Communicating Boundaries Confidently

Build confidence by practicing boundary-setting in advance (Fisher & Ury, 1981).

- **Role-playing**: Rehearse boundary-setting conversations with a mentor or friend. Practice saying no to unreasonable requests while maintaining professionalism.

- **Preparing Responses**: Anticipate difficult situations and plan your responses ahead of time. Being prepared empowers you to assert your boundaries confidently, whether at work or in personal situations.

You now have the tools to define and communicate your boundaries confidently. It's time to take action. As you move forward, assess how well you're implementing these techniques and identify areas where you can reinforce or adjust your boundaries. Each small step will bring you closer to mastering the art of protecting your space. This assessment will guide you through reflecting on your current boundary-setting practices and help you identify where you might need to reinforce or adjust your limits.

ASSESSMENT: BOUNDARY SETTING SCALE

Instructions: Rate each statement on a scale from 1 (Strongly disagree) to 5 (Strongly agree).

1. I clearly communicate my boundaries to others.
2. I feel confident in enforcing my boundaries.
3. I respect the boundaries of others.
4. I can recognize when my boundaries are being crossed.
5. I can adjust my boundaries as needed.
6. I feel comfortable discussing my boundaries with colleagues.
7. I can maintain my boundaries even under pressure.
8. I can handle conflicts that arise from boundary setting.
9. I regularly review and update my boundaries.
10. I feel empowered by setting and maintaining boundaries.

Scoring Interpretation

- 10-20: Low Boundary Setting Skills

   Description: Individuals in this range may struggle to communicate and enforce their boundaries. They might find it difficult to recognize when their boundaries are being crossed and feel uncomfortable discussing their boundaries with others.

Action Steps:

   1. Identify Personal Boundaries: Write down your personal boundaries and practice communicating them.

   2. Practice in Low-Stakes Situations: Start by setting boundaries in low-stakes situations to build confidence.

   3. Seek Support: Surround yourself with supportive people who respect your boundaries.

- 21-35: Moderate Boundary Setting Skills

Description: Individuals in this range have moderate boundary setting skills. They can communicate and enforce their boundaries in most situations but may still experience occasional discomfort or pressure.

Action Steps:

1. Role-Play Scenarios: Practice boundary-setting scenarios with a friend or mentor.

2. Reflect on Past Experiences: Think about past situations where you successfully set boundaries and what you can learn from them.

3. Reinforce Boundaries: Practice maintaining your boundaries even under pressure.

- 36-50: High Boundary Setting Skills

Description: Individuals in this range are highly skilled at setting and communicating boundaries. They feel confident in enforcing their boundaries and can handle conflicts that arise from boundary setting.

Action Steps:

1. Continue Enforcing Boundaries: Maintain your ability to set and communicate boundaries effectively.

2. Mentor Others: Help others develop their boundary-setting skills.

3. Reflect on Successes: Regularly reflect on your boundary-setting experiences and celebrate your successes.

Well done on mastering the ability to set and communicate your boundaries. You've now added a powerful layer to your professional toolkit—one that will protect your space, time, and energy. Establishing these boundaries is vital to maintaining your well-being and effectiveness at work.

Next, we'll tackle how to handle uncomfortable or inappropriate conversations, a crucial skill in protecting your professional image and maintaining a safe work environment. Get ready for **Chapter 4**, where we'll explore **navigating inappropriate conversations** with grace and authority.

04

NAVIGATING PROFESSIONALISM: MANAGING AND REDIRECTING INAPPROPRIATE CONVERSATIONS

"Balcony Boundaries: Steering Clear of Unwanted Advances"

I once worked for a powerful and influential boss who was going through a tough divorce. As his right-hand person, I was deeply involved in his day-to-day ventures, managing everything from business meetings to personal errands. Our professional relationship was built on mutual respect and trust, and I took pride in being a reliable support during his challenging times.

One evening, we found ourselves alone on a 36-foot balcony in Beverly Hills, overlooking the city lights. Though serene, the air felt heavy with unspoken tension. As we talked, he made a quick comment about how hard it was to move on and how he needed a woman in his life. His words hung in the air, and I sensed the potential for an uncomfortable situation.

Recognizing the need to steer the conversation back to a professional tone, I quickly responded, "I can help set you up on dating sites and even be the voice behind your profile, arranging dates for you to meet face-to-face." My goal was to remove myself from the category of potential romantic interest as swiftly as possible. By offering a practical solution, I aimed to defuse any inappropriate undertones and maintain our professional boundaries.

In situations like this, it's essential to assert that you are not an option. Hesitation or avoidance can lead to further inappropriate advances. By taking a firm stance and offering a professional alternative, I ensured that boundaries were maintained and the conversation remained appropriate. This approach protected my integrity and reinforced the importance of professionalism in the workplace.

This experience taught me a valuable lesson: professional boundaries must be clear and assertively upheld, especially in vulnerable moments. Let's explore how you can use this principle to navigate and redirect inappropriate conversations with confidence and control.

Steering Conversations Back on Track" When faced with inappropriate remarks, here are strategies to maintain professionalism and control the conversation (Goleman, 1995):

1. **Active Listening and Redirection**: Active Listening and Redirection: Acknowledge the comment, then redirect back to professionalism. For example, 'That's interesting, but let's refocus on [work-related topic].

2. **Finding Common Ground**: Use shared interests to shift the conversation naturally. If the discussion veers into uncomfortable territory, pivot by asking about neutral topics, like weekend plans or recent projects. This allows you to steer the conversation without creating tension (Scharff & Broidy, 1997).

3. **Using Humor to Defuse Tension**: A light, playful comment such as, "That's a bit off-topic, let's get back to business!" can help diffuse awkwardness while maintaining professionalism and keeping the conversation on track (Nilsen, 1993).

4. **Creating 'Topic Islands'**: Visualize safe, neutral subjects that you can easily return to when discussions go off-course. For exam-

ple, "Let's revisit the project details we talked about earlier." This technique keeps the conversation professional without confrontation (Peterson, 1999).

The 2 AM Code empowers women to navigate power dynamics without fear. It reminds us that regardless of who's in the room or what pressures are at play, we are entitled to respect. It's about staying grounded in your worth, even when facing those in authority, and asserting your voice with the strength that the Code provides.

The Story of Athena

Athena, the Greek goddess of wisdom and strategy, emerged fully grown and armored from the forehead of Zeus, symbolizing her innate power and intelligence (Graves, 1955). Revered for her strategic thinking and fairness, Athena was not just a warrior; she used intellect and wisdom to guide heroes like Odysseus through their toughest challenges. Athena shows us that true strength is a mix of wisdom and courage, and that navigating challenges, whether in battle or at work, requires strategy more than force.

Applying Athena's Lessons

In the professional world, like Athena, we must use intellect and strategy to confront challenges, especially when dealing with inappropriate conversations (Homer, 1980). Just as Athena wielded her shield for protection, we too must establish clear boundaries and communicate them with strength and wisdom.

The Wisdom of Athena: Strategies for Managing Inappropriate Conversations

Athena, the Greek goddess of wisdom and strategy, offers us timeless lessons in confronting challenges with intellect and strength. Her story reminds us that we, too, can employ strategy to manage and redirect uncomfortable conversations in professional settings.

1. **Direct Communication:** Like Athena's clear and strategic thinking, address inappropriate behavior head-on. Communicate how

the behavior impacts you and why professionalism must be upheld.

2. **Setting Boundaries:** Athena's shield symbolizes protection—your boundaries. Clearly state what is acceptable and what is not, and ensure these boundaries are upheld through personal and organizational standards.

3. **Seeking Support:** When direct communication doesn't work, seek allies, such as HR or a superior, to intervene. Athena knew when to ask for help, and so should we in creating a safe and respectful environment.

Historical Context of Professionalism and Inappropriate Conversations

In the early 20th century, male-dominated workplaces often overlooked or accepted inappropriate conversations (Jablin, 1987). However, as women gained more rights and workplace environments evolved, so did the expectation of professionalism. This shift underscores the importance of respectful communication and the necessity of addressing inappropriate behavior proactively.

Perspectives and Points of View

Employee Perspective: Employees may fear speaking up about inappropriate conversations, worried about retaliation or exclusion. It's essential to foster a safe and supportive environment where concerns can be voiced without fear (Goffman, 1967).

Management Perspective: Managers must lead by example and address inappropriate behavior consistently, creating a culture where boundaries are respected, and professionalism is maintained (Mintzberg, 1973).

Navigating Sexual Conversations

- Understanding Context: Begin by assessing the setting in which the conversation is taking place (Fisher & Ury, 1981). If it's a workplace or a formal setting, point out the importance of maintaining professionalism. Highlight that contextual awareness allows for a more effective redirect.

- Verbal Cues and Body Language: Discuss the importance of non-verbal communication. If someone turns the topic sexual, gently shift your body away or maintain an open, neutral posture. Use verbal cues like "That's an interesting perspective, but what do you think about [insert a neutral topic]?"

- Setting Boundaries: Introduce the concept of expressing discomfort about certain topics. For example, you might say, "I prefer discussions that focus on work-related subjects," which sets clear boundaries without confronting the person harshly.

- Redirecting the Conversation: Provide phrases such as, "I'm not comfortable discussing that. Have you heard about [insert an appropriate topic]?" This technique allows for a smooth transition away from anything inappropriate while maintaining the flow of conversation.

As you've learned, effectively navigating inappropriate conversations requires tact, clear boundaries, and confidence in your communication skills. However, beyond mastering these techniques, true success lies in understanding the emotions at play—both yours and those of others. This is where emotional intelligence becomes an essential tool. By harnessing emotional intelligence, you not only assert your boundaries but do so with empathy, ensuring that your interactions remain professional and respectful, even in challenging situations."

Harnessing Emotional Intelligence for Effective Boundaries

Emotional intelligence is a critical asset in setting and maintaining boundaries. Awareness of your own and others' emotions lets you navigate difficult conversations with empathy and ease (Goleman, 1995).

Self-Awareness: Recognize when a conversation makes you uncomfortable and why. This awareness allows you to assert boundaries confidently.

1. **Self-Regulation:** Control your emotional responses during difficult conversations. Stay calm and composed, even when the other person is challenging your boundaries.

2. **Empathy:** Understand the other person's perspective while still asserting your needs. This balance fosters mutual respect.

3. **Social Skills:** Use strong communication skills to reinforce boundaries without damaging relationships. Ensure that conversations remain respectful and focused on professionalism.

Professionalism isn't just about rules—it's about asserting boundaries and maintaining control with grace. Now that you have the tools to handle these conversations, use the following assessment to reflect on your progress and areas for growth.

ASSESSMENT: INAPPROPRIATE DISCUSSION MANAGEMENT SCALE

Instructions: Rate each statement on a scale from 1 (Strongly disagree) to 5 (Strongly agree).

1. I can recognize when a discussion becomes inappropriate.
2. I feel confident in redirecting inappropriate conversations.
3. I can address inappropriate comments assertively.
4. I know how to report inappropriate behavior if necessary.
5. I can maintain professionalism in uncomfortable situations.
6. I am aware of the policies regarding inappropriate discussions at my workplace.
7. I can provide feedback to colleagues about inappropriate comments.
8. I can handle emotional reactions during inappropriate discussions.
9. I can support colleagues who are affected by inappropriate discussions.
10. I can create a respectful and inclusive work environment.

Scoring Interpretation

- 10-20: Low Ability to Manage Inappropriate Discussions

   Description: Individuals in this range may struggle to recognize and address inappropriate discussions. They might feel uncomfortable redirecting conversations and lack confidence in reporting inappropriate behavior.

Action Steps:

   1. Learn to Identify Signs: Educate yourself on the signs of inappropriate discussions.

2. Practice Redirecting Conversations: Practice redirecting conversations in a safe environment.

3. Familiarize Yourself with Policies: Learn about your workplace's policies on inappropriate discussions and reporting procedures.

- 21-35: Moderate Ability to Manage Inappropriate Discussions

Description: Individuals in this range have a moderate ability to manage inappropriate discussions. They can recognize and address inappropriate comments in most situations but may still experience occasional discomfort.

Action Steps:

1. Develop Assertive Communication Skills: Practice assertive communication to address inappropriate comments confidently.

2. Reflect on Past Experiences: Think about past situations where you managed inappropriate discussions and what you can learn from them.

3. Seek Support: Surround yourself with supportive colleagues who can provide guidance.

- 36-50: High Ability to Manage Inappropriate Discussions

Description: Individuals in this range are highly skilled at managing inappropriate discussions. They can recognize and address inappropriate comments assertively and maintain professionalism in uncomfortable situations.

Action Steps:

1. Continue Managing Effectively: Maintain your ability to handle inappropriate discussions confidently.

2. Mentor Others: Help others develop their skills in managing inappropriate discussions.

3. Reflect on Successes: Regularly reflect on your experiences and celebrate your effective handling of inappropriate discussions.

You've successfully learned how to manage and redirect uncomfortable conversations, a skill that will enhance your ability to maintain professionalism and uphold your boundaries. These techniques equip you to handle even the most awkward situations with confidence and composure.

Next, we'll shift our focus to understanding interpersonal dynamics, particularly the **male ego** in the workplace. In **Chapter 5**, we'll uncover insights into how this dynamic shapes professional interactions and how you can navigate them effectively. Let's explore **decoding the male ego** for more productive workplace relationships.

05

DECODING THE MALE EGO: INSIGHTS FOR PROFESSIONAL INTERACTIONS

The Silent Sacrifice: Navigating Ethical Dilemmas in High-Stakes Events"

The Cost of Compliance: Navigating Ethical Dilemmas

From the moment I accepted the role of managing a high-profile weekend event for elite masterminds—each attendee paying $25,000—I knew the stakes were sky-high. Everything had to be flawless: airport pickups, meal arrangements, and the overall experience had to exceed every expectation. The pressure was immense, but I took pride in orchestrating every detail with precision. This was my moment to shine, to prove that I could handle anything.

But as dinner approached, a pit formed in my stomach. I had hired a phenomenal team to serve the group of 12 to 16 influential men—each staff member carefully selected for their professionalism and efficiency. But they were all male. My boss, a man notorious for his exacting standards and volatile temper, stormed toward me, his face flushed with rage. His voice escalated with each word, sharp and biting.

"What the F are you doing? You hired all men—and a ton of gay men—to serve these guys? I don't want them here."

Despite the staff's flawless work, I found myself apologizing, not because I believed I had done anything wrong, but because the power dynamic left me no choice. I could feel my integrity slipping away as I nodded along, the injustice of the situation clawing at me. But the need to ensure the event's success—and avoid further wrath from my boss—kept me from standing my ground.

The order was clear: send them home. Replace them with female staff the next day. I felt sick. I knew this was biased, unethical, and deeply unfair, yet I complied. My hands tied, I made the call.

That night, I sat in my car, the weight of my decision crushing me. Tears streamed down my face as the gravity of what I'd done hit me full force. I had compromised my values. The professionalism I had so carefully maintained throughout the event was overshadowed by my compliance in an unfair practice. I had allowed someone else's prejudice to dictate my actions, and that realization tore me apart.

I confided in a coworker, someone I trusted. But even in my vulnerability, I hesitated—I had always been the strong one, the unshakeable force. Yet here I was, unraveling. This was the harsh reality of ethical dilemmas: sometimes, in the heat of the moment, the pressure to meet expectations can eclipse your own moral compass.

That moment became a turning point in my career. It was a painful lesson, but one I would never forget: no matter how high the stakes, no success is worth sacrificing your values. Standing up for what is right—especially in the face of pressure and authority—is the only way to maintain true self-respect. It was in that realization that I found my strength

Catering to Male Ego

The 2 AM Code empowers women to balance professionalism with personal integrity, reinforcing that you never have to compromise your principles or comfort to succeed in a male-dominated space.

Understanding the male ego's influence on workplace dynamics is essential for fostering collaboration without compromising your integrity (Eagly & Carli, 2007). A healthy male ego drives ambition and leadership, while an inflated or fragile ego can trigger defensive reactions, making collaboration and feedback challenging. Let's explore the psychological aspects of the male ego to better navigate these interactions and maintain balanced professional relationships.

Psychological Aspects of the Male Ego

The male ego is shaped by both psychological and societal pressures. Internally, it is driven by personal thoughts, emotions, and needs, where a healthy ego promotes confidence, while an inflated or fragile one can lead to defensiveness (Horney, 1937). Externally, societal expectations and peer feedback influence men's sense of self-worth, often pressuring them to conform to standards of dominance and success (Connell, 2005).

In the workplace, the male ego can manifest in various ways, influencing interactions, decision-making, and overall team dynamics. The male ego can influence workplace dynamics in both positive and negative ways. On the positive side, a healthy ego fosters confidence, ambition, and leadership, driving men to take on challenges, pursue ambitious goals, and encourage innovation through risk-taking. However, when the ego is inflated, it can lead to arrogance, making it difficult to accept feedback or collaborate effectively. Men with fragile egos may react defensively to criticism, potentially creating a hostile work environment. Additionally, an excessive focus on personal achievement can undermine teamwork and breed conflict, prioritizing competition over collaboration.

Men's perceptions and behaviors are deeply shaped by socialization patterns that begin in early childhood. From a young age, boys are conditoned to be strong, assertive, and competitive, with gender roles reinforced through toys, media, and societal expectations. Cultural norms further emphasize traits like independence, dominance, and emotional restraint, shaping how men view themselves and their roles in society. Peer groups also play a crucial role, as men may feel pressured to conform to group expectations to gain acceptance and respect. Together, these factors significantly influence how men navigate both personal and professional interactions.

Balancing Power Dynamics in the Workplace

Understanding the male ego helps us better navigate power dynamics in hierarchical relationships. Whether dealing with a superior or managing a team, balancing assertiveness with empathy is key. Be clear about your role and responsibilities, communicate respectfully, and seek feedback to ensure alignment (Kanter, 1977). These practices allow you to assert influence while maintaining professional boundaries and mutual respect.

Successfully balancing power dynamics requires not only understanding the male ego but also knowing how to navigate hierarchical relationships with confidence and respect. Let's explore specific strategies that can help you assert your influence while maintaining professionalism and mutual respect.

Navigating Hierarchical Relationships

In hierarchical relationships, it's important to navigate power dynamics carefully to maintain professionalism and mutual respect. Here are some strategies:

1. Understand Your Role: Be clear about your responsibilities and the scope of your authority. This helps in setting boundaries and understanding where you can assert influence (Goleman, 1995) .

2. Communicate Effectively: Use clear and respectful communication to express your ideas and concerns. Active listening and empathy are key to understanding others' perspectives and building strong relationships (Scharff & Broidy, 1997).

3. Seek Feedback: Regularly seek feedback from colleagues and superiors to understand how your actions are perceived and to identify areas for improvement (Hogan & Kaiser, 2005).

As you navigate power dynamics, your ability to communicate clearly and set boundaries is essential. These skills also play a crucial role when affirming your confidence and authority in professional settings.

This is where the 2 AM Code becomes critical—it's a reminder that you don't need to compromise your integrity or confidence to fit into any professional space. In the next section, we'll explore how you can affirm your own confidence without overstepping or losing your position, using the strength of the 2 AM Code as a foundation for maintaining both respect and authority.

Affirming Confidence Without Compromising Position

Affirming confidence is essential in the workplace, but it's important to do so while maintaining professionalism (Rudman, 1998). Here's how to strike that balance:

1. **Acknowledge Achievements**: Celebrate accomplishments, both yours and your team's, through meetings, emails, or informal conversations.

    ▫ As an illustration: 'The work you did on this project was outstanding. Your attention to detail made a real difference."

2. **Provide Constructive Feedback**: Give specific, actionable feedback that fosters professional growth (Carnegie, 1936).

    ▫ For instance: 'Great presentation! Next time, consider adding more visual aids to enhance your points.."

3. **Use Positive Affirmations**: Incorporate daily affirmations to boost both your confidence and others (Covey, 1989).

    ▫ Such as: 'I'm confident in my abilities and ready to take on new challenges."

4. **Maintain Professional Boundaries**: Keep praise professional and avoid personal compliments that could be misinterpreted.

    ▫ As a case in point: 'Your leadership on this project has been exceptional, driving the team's success.."

5. **Choose the Right Timing**: Offer praise and affirmations at appropriate moments, such as after key accomplishments or during reviews, to ensure authenticity.

Just as you balance confidence with professional boundaries, interactions that blur the line between personal and professional—like flirting—require similar vigilance. Let's explore how you can maintain your professional integrity while navigating these tricky dynamics.

Flirting While Maintaining Professionalism

Defining Flirting

Flirting has long been a part of human interaction, but in today's workplace, it requires careful management (Goffman, 1959). While light conversation can foster positive connections, it's important to understand the boundaries between friendliness and professionalism.

The Fine Line of Flirting in the Workplace

In the modern workplace, flirting can tread a fine line between acceptable social interaction and inappropriate behavior. While playful banter and respectful compliments can foster positive connections when consensual, flirting becomes problematic when it crosses boundaries, causes discomfort, or creates a hostile environment.

Understanding the delicate balance between friendliness and professionalism requires being mindful of the power dynamics at play. The key is ensuring that all interactions are grounded in mutual respect and consent. This is particularly important in workplace settings where personal boundaries must be honored to create a culture of safety and inclusivity. Professional integrity should never be compromised for personal interactions.

Appropriate vs. Inappropriate Flirting

- **Appropriate Flirting**: Consensual, light-hearted interactions that are respectful and enjoyable for both parties. It might include compliments, friendly teasing, or casual conversation.

- **Inappropriate Flirting**: Any behavior that is unwelcome, persistent, or makes someone uncomfortable. This could involve suggestive comments, unwanted physical contact, or behavior that undermines professionalism.

Guidelines for Flirting and Maintaining Professionalism

Navigating personal interactions at work requires sensitivity and respect for boundaries. Here are key principles to ensure flirting doesn't undermine your professional integrity:

1. **Understand Company Policies**: Make sure you are familiar with your organization's policies regarding workplace relationships. Adhering to these rules helps prevent misunderstandings and maintains a professional atmosphere.

2. **Set Clear Boundaries**: Establish and maintain respectful boundaries in your interactions. Ensure that your behavior is never perceived as inappropriate or uncomfortable.

3. **Prioritize Professionalism**: Focus on your responsibilities and maintain a professional demeanor, even during personal interactions. Ensure that any personal exchanges don't interfere with your job performance.

4. **Communicate Discreetly**: If you have a personal interest in a colleague, communicate respectfully and ensure their comfort. Always be mindful of boundaries to avoid crossing into inappropriate territory.

5. **Seek Guidance if Needed**: If you are ever uncertain about the appropriateness of your behavior, seek advice from HR or a trusted mentor to avoid crossing any lines.

As we've explored the importance of maintaining professionalism in personal interactions, it's crucial to recognize the fine line between appropriate and inappropriate behavior. Flirting, when done respectfully, should never compromise your integrity or workplace boundaries.

Next, we'll dive into practical techniques to help you navigate these interactions with confidence, ensuring your actions remain respectful and aligned with professional standards. Let's look at how to strike the right balance between personal dynamics and professionalism.

Professional Flirting Techniques

Navigating personal interactions in the workplace, particularly in hierarchical relationships, requires a delicate balance of professionalism, respect, and self-awareness (Tannen, 1990). Understanding your role and asserting your boundaries are crucial for maintaining a positive dynamic without overstepping. Clear, respectful communication allows you to express your needs and intentions while fostering a collaborative environment where everyone's voice is respected. Seeking feedback regularly also helps ensure you align with professional expectations and that your value is recognized.

Equally important is knowing when to step back. Paying attention to both verbal and non-verbal cues is essential—if the other person seems uncomfortable, disengaged, or hesitant, it's a signal to withdraw gracefully. Always respect personal and professional boundaries, avoiding any remarks or behaviors that could be misinterpreted or undermine your professional standing. Attuning yourself to these signals not only protects your reputation but reinforces your commitment to maintaining a respectful, professional atmosphere.

Understanding these dynamics—particularly when the male ego, assertiveness, or competition are in play—allows you to navigate professional relationships with both confidence and empathy. By managing interactions carefully, you ensure that your boundaries are honored while creating an environment where others feel respected and valued.

In environments often shaped by gender bias, **The 2 AM Code** *empowers you to assert your presence without compromising your values. Whether negotiating a contract or reinforcing your boundaries at a company event, the Code serves as a reminder that your worth isn't dependent on external approval. You are not just there to survive, but to thrive, and your contributions are as valid and valuable as anyone else's. This philosophy empowers you to maintain your professionalism and integrity in every interaction, creating a workplace where your voice is heard and your presence respected.*

Navigating Compliments and Attention in the Workplace

Socialization patterns heavily influence how men perceive compliments and attention, often tying them to affirmations of competence and status (Kimmel, 1996). Compliments can serve as a boost to self-esteem, but if a compliment challenges their self-image or comes from someone seen as a rival, it may trigger discomfort or suspicion. Similarly, positive attention can enhance a man's sense of importance and competence, while negative attention or criticism may threaten their self-esteem, leading to defensive reactions.

Understanding this dynamic is key to navigating professional interactions. Subtle, well-timed compliments focused on professional achievements and specific skills help maintain a balance, boosting confidence without overstepping boundaries.

Examples of Subtle Compliments:

1. **Professional Achievements:**

   - "Your presentation was incredibly insightful—it really clarified the project's direction" (Goffman, 1959).

   - "The way you handled that client meeting was impressive. Your negotiation skills are top-notch."

   - "Your leadership on this project has been outstanding. The team's success is a testament to your guidance."

2. **Specific Skills:**

   - "Your attention to detail is remarkable. It's enhanced the overall quality of our work" (Tannen, 1990).

   - "I admire your problem-solving skills—you always find effective solutions quickly."

   - "Your creativity brings fresh ideas to the table. It's inspiring to see your innovative approach."

Timing and Context Matter:

1. **Consider the Recipient**: Tailor your compliment to the individual's role and contributions. For example, recognize a manager for their leadership or a peer for their teamwork.

2. **Be Specific**: Avoid vague praise like "Good job." Instead, offer a detailed compliment such as, "Good job on the presentation. Your ability to clearly explain the material was truly enlightening."

3. **Offer Timely Praise**: Compliment soon after an achievement for maximum impact. Acknowledging effort immediately after a challenging task boosts morale.

4. **Keep It Professional**: Focus on work-related achievements and skills, not personal attributes, to maintain appropriate boundaries.

5. **Match the Tone**: Ensure your language fits the workplace culture—whether formal or casual, always keep it respectful and professional.

Completing the male ego awareness assessment will give you greater insight into your strengths and areas for growth, helping you better navigate power dynamics, enhance communication, and assert your leadership confidently. Let's move forward and unlock the next stage of your growth."

ASSESSMENT: MALE EGO AWARENESS SCALE

Instructions: Rate each statement on a scale from 1 (Strongly disagree) to 5 (Strongly agree).

1. I understand how the male ego can influence workplace dynamics.

2. I can recognize behaviors driven by the male ego.

3. I feel confident in navigating interactions influenced by the male ego.

4. I can address ego-driven behaviors effectively.

5. I can maintain my composure in ego-driven situations.

6. I am aware of the impact of the male ego on team dynamics.

7. I can identify when the male ego is affecting decision-making.

8. I can communicate effectively with colleagues who exhibit strong ego-driven behaviors.

9. I can provide constructive feedback to colleagues with strong egos.

10. I can foster a collaborative environment despite ego-driven challenges.

Scoring Interpretation

- 10-20: Low Awareness of the Male Ego

Description: Individuals in this range may have limited understanding of how the male ego influences workplace dynamics. They might struggle to recognize ego-driven behaviors and feel unprepared to navigate interactions influenced by the male ego.

Action Steps:

1. Educate Yourself: Learn about the concept of the male ego and its impact on workplace dynamics.

2. Observe Interactions: Pay attention to interactions in the workplace to identify ego-driven behaviors.

3. Seek Feedback: Ask trusted colleagues for feedback on how you handle ego-driven situations.

- 21-35: Moderate Awareness of the Male Ego

Description: Individuals in this range have a moderate understanding of the male ego and its impact. They can recognize ego-driven behaviors and navigate most interactions but may still experience occasional challenges.

Action Steps:

1. Practice Strategies: Develop and practice strategies for addressing ego-driven behaviors.

2. Reflect on Past Experiences: Think about past interactions influenced by the male ego and what you can learn from them.

3. Seek Mentorship: Find a mentor who can provide guidance on navigating ego-driven dynamics.

- 36-50: High Awareness of the Male Ego

Description: Individuals in this range have a strong understanding of the male ego and its influence on workplace dynamics. They can effectively navigate interactions influenced by the male ego and address ego-driven behaviors confidently.

Action Steps:

1. Continue Navigating Effectively: Maintain your ability to handle ego-driven interactions.

2. Share Insights: Help others understand and manage the male ego by sharing your insights.

3. Reflect on Successes: Regularly reflect on your experiences and celebrate your effective handling of ego-driven situations.

You've completed a deep dive into the complexities of the male ego in professional settings. With your newfound understanding, you can navigate these dynamics with confidence, empathy, and clarity, fostering more productive relationships while maintaining your own empowerment.

Next, we'll focus on another crucial aspect of professional communication: **nonverbal cues**, specifically eye contact. Join me in **Chapter 6** as we explore how mastering eye contact can significantly enhance your professional presence and impact.

CHAPTER

06

THE SILENT COMMUNICATOR: MASTERING EYE CONTACT FOR PROFESSIONAL IMPACT

Instincts in Hollywood: A Night to Remember"

The Hollywood Escape

One unforgettable night, I found myself partying with some of the biggest names in Hollywood at one of the most luxurious mansions in Los Angeles. The air was electric with glamour and excitement, the kind of night that felt like a scene from a movie. Celebrities mingled with industry insiders, and the atmosphere was charged with the promise of unforgettable memories.

As the evening wound down, my boss decided to send a few of us to a hotel room he had been given, likely as a complimentary perk. We all piled into an Uber and headed to the hotel, the car filled with laughter and the buzz of the night's events. By the time we arrived, it was late, and we had all been drinking. Despite the alcohol, I remained aware of my surroundings, knowing I needed to relax but also stay vigilant.

Once we got to the room, I assessed the situation: one male assistant and three female colleagues. The room was spacious but lacked enough comfortable places for everyone to rest. I felt a growing sense of unease about staying. The combination of alcohol, the late hour, and the mixed company made me wary.

Without drawing attention, I quietly ordered an Uber. When it arrived, I announced, "My Uber is here," and left immediately, ensuring I got home safely to my husband and children. The next morning, I learned that the male assistant had made inappropriate advances towards one of my colleagues. My decision to leave early had been the right one, avoiding a potentially dangerous and unprofessional situation.

This experience reinforced not only the importance of trusting my instincts but also how non-verbal cues, such as eye contact, can influence professional interactions. In moments where words may fail or escalate a situation, non-verbal communication becomes your most powerful tool.

Understanding Non-Verbal Communication

Eye contact is a key element of nonverbal communication that plays a crucial role in shaping social interactions and professional relationships (Argyle, 1972). Effectively using eye contact can help you connect with others, convey confidence, and build trust. Here's why eye contact matters:

1. **Building Trust and Credibility**: Maintaining eye contact signals honesty and confidence, helping to establish trust and making you appear more credible and reliable (Burgoon et al., 1996).

2. **Enhancing Communication**: Eye contact shows engagement and attentiveness, demonstrating interest and understanding, which makes conversations more meaningful (Knapp & Hall, 2009).

3. **Influencing Perceptions**: Appropriate eye contact makes you appear more confident, competent, and approachable, positively influencing how others perceive you in professional settings (Hartenstein, 2002).

4. **Regulating Conversations**: Eye contact helps manage the flow of conversation, signaling when it's your turn to speak or listen,

making communication smoother and more effective (Philpot, 2001).

Historical Significance of Eye Contact

Eye contact has played a crucial role in human interactions throughout history. Here are some historical insights:

Ancient Civilizations: In ancient Greece and Rome, eye contact was considered a sign of respect and attentiveness. Philosophers like Aristotle emphasized the importance of eye contact in rhetoric and public speaking (Aristotle, Rhetoric) .

Cultural Variations: Different cultures have varied norms regarding eye contact. For example, in many Western cultures, direct eye contact is associated with confidence and honesty, while in some Asian cultures, prolonged eye contact can be seen as confrontational or disrespectful (Hall, 1966).

Evolutionary Perspective: From an evolutionary standpoint, eye contact has been essential for social bonding and communication. It helps convey emotions and intentions, facilitating cooperation and social cohesion (Tomasello, 2008).

To effectively use eye contact in professional settings, maintain steady but non-intense eye contact to show attentiveness and create an inclusive atmosphere. In group dynamics, make eye contact with various participants to encourage engagement and ensure everyone feels valued. Combine eye contact with positive body language like open posture and subtle mirroring to build rapport. Show genuine interest by asking open-ended questions, actively listening, and offering specific compliments. Use humor to ease tension and make eye contact feel natural. Finally, know when to withdraw by reading verbal and non-verbal cues to maintain professionalism and respect personal boundaries.

With a deeper understanding of how eye contact has influenced human interaction throughout history, let's now explore specific techniques to apply this knowledge in today's professional environments.

The Power of Non-Verbal Cues:

Nonverbal communication is a powerful tool in professional interactions, influencing perceptions, building relationships, and conveying messages without words. Let's explore the key aspects of nonverbal communication, its role in expressing confidence and authority, and the importance of cultural considerations.

Nonverbal Communication

Nonverbal communication involves a variety of behaviors and signals that convey meaning beyond words (Mehrabian, 1981). These cues—such as facial expressions, gestures, posture, eye contact, and tone of voice—play a vital role in how we connect with others, communicate messages, and build professional relationships. Mastering these nonverbal elements can greatly enhance your interactions and strengthen connections.

Key elements of nonverbal communication include:

- **Facial Expressions:** These instantly convey emotions like happiness, surprise, anger, or sadness. For example, a smile signals friendliness, while a frown can indicate disapproval (Ekman & Friesen, 1969).

- **Gestures:** Hand movements, nods, or shakes of the head emphasize points, indicate agreement or disagreement, and help direct the flow of conversation (Pease & Pease, 2004).

- **Posture and Body Language:** Standing tall with your shoulders back exudes confidence, while slouching or closed-off body language can suggest insecurity or lack of interest (Givens, 2005).

- **Eye Contact:** Steady eye contact shows attentiveness and engagement, while avoiding it may signal discomfort or a lack of confidence (Kleinke, 1986).

- **Tone of Voice:** Variations in pitch, volume, and pace can convey enthusiasm, urgency, or calmness, helping to reinforce the intent behind your words (Brennan, 2007).

Non-verbal communication shapes how others perceive you. In professional environments, mastering these cues isn't just about sending the right signals—it's about projecting confidence and authority, key elements for building a strong presence.

Confidence & Authority

Projecting confidence and authority through nonverbal cues is essential in professional settings. How you carry yourself—through eye contact, posture, gestures, and tone—directly impacts how others perceive you (Goleman, 1995). Using these signals effectively allows you to assert your presence, command respect, and create a lasting, positive impression.

Key nonverbal cues for confidence and authority include:

- **Eye Contact**: Steady eye contact shows confidence and builds trust, signaling that you are engaged and reliable.
- **Posture**: Standing tall with open body language communicates confidence and authority. Avoid crossed arms or slouching, as these can suggest defensiveness or insecurity.
- **Gestures**: Purposeful gestures can emphasize your points and convey control. Limit fidgeting, as it may detract from your message.
- **Facial Expressions**: A composed expression, paired with appropriate smiles, enhances both credibility and approachability.
- **Tone of Voice**: A clear, steady voice conveys confidence and helps maintain attention, ensuring your message resonates effectively.

Cultural Considerations

Being mindful of these differences can enhance your ability to navigate diverse workplace environments and build stronger connections. Awareness of cultural variations in nonverbal cues such as eye contact, gestures, personal space, facial expressions, and touch is crucial in preventing misunderstandings that could undermine professional relationships. In a global or diverse professional setting, adapting your nonverbal communication to align with cultural norms not only fosters respect but also promotes more effective and inclusive interactions, ensuring that your message is conveyed with clarity and confidence across different cultures.

Nonverbal communication varies significantly across cultures, and understanding these differences is essential for effective intercultural interactions:

- Gestures: Common gestures in one culture may have different meanings in another. For example, a thumbs-up gesture is positive in many Western cultures but can be offensive in parts of the Middle East.

- Personal Space: The acceptable distance between individuals during conversations varies by culture. In some cultures, close proximity is normal, while in others, maintaining a greater distance is preferred.

- Facial Expressions: The interpretation of facial expressions can differ. For instance, in some cultures, smiling may not always indicate happiness but could be used to mask discomfort or embarrassment.

- Touch: The appropriateness of physical touch, such as handshakes or pats on the back, varies widely. Understanding these norms is crucial to avoid misunderstandings.

Being mindful of cultural differences in non-verbal communication is key to fostering professional respect (Hall, 1966). In addition to understanding these variations, knowing when to strategically limit eye contact can help you navigate difficult situations and assert control when needed.

Limiting Eye Contact Strategically

While eye contact can enhance your presence, it can also become a double-edged sword in certain situations, particularly when dealing with inappropriate advances or tension (Burgoon et al., 1996). Knowing when and how to limit eye contact is essential for maintaining professionalism and setting boundaries effectively.

When to Limit Eye Contact:

- **In High-Tension Situations:** If someone is making you uncomfortable, subtly lowering your gaze can signal disinterest without escalating the situation. This simple shift can help you regain control and defuse the interaction.

- **Conversations with Certain Individuals:** If you've noticed a pattern of unwanted attention or advances from specific colleagues or superiors, limiting eye contact can help discourage their behavior and reduce any unintended encouragement.

Pairing with Body Language:

Combine limited eye contact with other body language signals to reinforce your disinterest. Crossing your arms or turning your body slightly away can create a physical barrier that conveys boundaries without the need for confrontation.

- **Balancing Eye Contact:** While limiting eye contact is important in specific scenarios, it's equally crucial to balance your overall use of it. Eye contact should be steady but not intense, as prolonged staring can be perceived as aggressive or confrontational.

- **Varying Durations:** Aim for a balanced approach—hold eye contact for a few seconds, then break it by looking away briefly. This cyclical method keeps the conversation comfortable and avoids creating discomfort.

- **Incorporating Positive Body Language:** Combine eye contact with gestures such as nodding or leaning slightly forward. These actions show engagement and openness, helping to establish rapport without appearing overly assertive.

- **Navigating Confidence in Eye Contact:** For women navigating male-dominated fields, balancing eye contact can be especially important. Gender biases, exclusion from key networks, and stereotypes often pressure women to downplay their presence. This can contribute to feelings of imposter syndrome or self-doubt, making it even more vital to use eye contact consciously to assert authority while maintaining boundaries.

While limiting eye contact is crucial in specific scenarios, consistently applying effective eye contact techniques can enhance your overall professional presence. Let's now look at practical tips to refine your use of eye contact across all interactions.

Practical Tips for Effective Eye Contact

- Follow the 50/70 Rule: Aim to maintain eye contact for about 50% of the time while listening and about 70% of the time while speaking (Knapp & Hall, 2009). This ratio fosters engagement without crossing into discomfort.

- Utilize Eye Contact as a Tool for Influence: Positive eye contact can enhance your persuasiveness. When making a point in a discussion or negotiation, look your audience in the eye to reinforce your confidence and belief in what you're saying.

- Practice with the "Three-Point Gazing" Technique: When presenting to a group, divide the audience into three sections (left, center, right) and make eye contact with individuals in each section throughout your speech (Pease & Pease, 2004). This method helps create a sense of connection with the group while also distributing your attention evenly.

As we saw in the Hollywood escape, knowing when to trust your instincts and communicate silently is as important as the words we speak. Mastering non-verbal communication, especially eye contact, allows you to convey authority, respect, and boundaries without saying a word. The 2 AM Code is not just about vocal assertiveness—it's about owning every form of communication, silent or spoken. Through these skills, you can navigate professional spaces with confidence, and now, the following assessment will help you further refine your ability to master silent cues for even greater impact.

ASSESSMENT: EYE CONTACT COMFORT SCALE

Instructions: Rate each statement on a scale from 1 (Strongly disagree) to 5 (Strongly agree).

1. I feel comfortable maintaining eye contact during conversations.
2. I use eye contact to show interest and engagement.
3. I can hold eye contact without feeling anxious.
4. I notice when others avoid eye contact.
5. I use eye contact to convey confidence.
6. I can read emotions through eye contact.
7. I feel more connected to people when I maintain eye contact.
8. I use eye contact to emphasize important points.
9. I am aware of cultural differences in eye contact norms.
10. I can maintain eye contact even in challenging conversations.

Scoring Interpretation

- 10-20: Low Comfort with Eye Contact

Description: Individuals in this range may feel anxious or uncomfortable maintaining eye contact. They might avoid eye contact during conversations and struggle to use it effectively to convey confidence and engagement.

Action Steps:

1. Practice in Front of a Mirror: Maintain eye contact with yourself in the mirror to build comfort.

2. Gradually Increase Duration: Start with brief eye contact and gradually increase the duration in conversations.

3. Observe Confident Communicators: Watch how confident people use eye contact and try to emulate their behavior.

- 21-35: Moderate Comfort with Eye Contact

Description: Individuals in this range are moderately comfortable with eye contact. They can maintain eye contact in most situations but may still experience occasional discomfort. They use eye contact to show interest and engagement but might struggle in challenging conversations.

Action Steps:

1. Use Eye Contact to Emphasize Points: Practice using eye contact to highlight important points in discussions.

2. Reflect on Interactions: Think about past interactions where you used eye contact effectively and what you can learn from them.

3. Increase Eye Contact in Challenging Situations: Gradually practice maintaining eye contact in more challenging conversations.

- 36-50: High Comfort with Eye Contact

Description: Individuals in this range are highly comfortable with eye contact. They use it effectively to convey confidence, show interest, and engage with others. They can maintain eye contact even in challenging conversations and are aware of cultural differences in eye contact norms.

Action Steps:

1. Continue Using Eye Contact Effectively: Maintain your use of eye contact in all interactions.

2. Teach Others: Share the importance of eye contact with others and help them develop their skills.

3. Reflect on Successes: Regularly reflect on your interactions and celebrate your effective use of eye contact.

As you complete the assessment and reflect on your mastery of non-verbal cues, remember that eye contact and body language are powerful tools in shaping your professional presence. Whether asserting authority or navigating complex dynamics, these silent signals allow you to communicate confidence, set boundaries, and build trust without speaking a word. Now that you've honed your understanding of silent communication, it's time to dive into another critical aspect of professional influence: managing difficult conversations with grace. In Chapter 7, we'll explore strategies for turning challenging interactions into opportunities for growth and assertive leadership. Let's move forward together.

07

THE POWER OF PERCEPTION: MANAGING APPEARANCE IN PROFESSIONAL SETTINGS

The Unintended Comment: A Lesson in Professional Boundaries

During my time as a salesperson, I was tasked with inspecting warehouses to ensure they met our company's stringent standards. This role required a keen eye for detail and the ability to assess both the physical environment and the personnel managing it. One day, I was given a tour by the warehouse supervisor, a man who clearly took great care of his physique. His dedication to fitness was evident, and it was clear he took pride in his appearance.

As we walked through the facility, discussing the type of individuals best suited for the job, I made an offhand comment that I immediately regretted. I said, "Well, I'll tell you right now, none of the guys will look like you." The moment the words left my mouth, I realized my mistake. The supervisor's expression shifted from professional to slightly uncomfortable, and I felt a wave of embarrassment and regret wash over me.

My intention was never to make him uncomfortable or to imply that physical appearance was a criterion for the job. Yet, in that instant, I had inadvertently crossed a line. As a woman, I understood the implications of my comment. It could have been perceived as sexually suggestive and inappropriate, opening the door for unwanted responses or advances. I had to take responsibility for my actions and recognize that, while the compliment was meant to be harmless, it was inappropriate in a professional setting.

By suggesting that the men we hired wouldn't be as buff or fit as the supervisor, I inadvertently reinforced stereotypes and made an unfair comparison. This realization hit me hard. I knew that professionalism required more than just competence in my tasks; it also demanded a high level of awareness and sensitivity in my interactions.

This moment made me realize just how powerful perceptions can be in the workplace. Our appearance and words carry weight, influencing the way others view us, even when we don't realize it. Let's explore how appearance and perception play critical roles in shaping professional success.

Understanding Appearance, Perception, and Nonverbal Communication

Our appearance and the perceptions others form about us hold significant weight in the workplace, influencing everything from first impressions to long-term professional relationships. The psychological impact of appearance can shape how we are treated, the opportunities we receive, and even our career trajectory. Research highlights that visual characteristics, including facial appearance, play a crucial role in judgments and decisions in professional settings. For example, the "halo effect" suggests that attractive individuals are often perceived more favorably, where positive traits are attributed based on looks alone (Dion et al., 1972). This demonstrates the importance of being mindful of our appearance and how it shapes others' perceptions.

However, the 2 AM Code emphasizes that true leadership comes from authenticity. It's not about conforming to perceptions but about leading confidently from a place of self-awareness and integrity. While it's easy to assume that first impressions are out of our control, understanding the psychology behind appearance gives you a distinct advantage. You can actively manage how you're perceived, reinforcing your leadership presence with authenticity, instead of allowing unconscious biases to take the lead (Todorov et al., 2005).

First Impressions and Nonverbal Communication

Equally important to appearance is nonverbal communication, which works hand-in-hand with your words to influence how you're perceived. Nonverbal cues such as facial expressions, gestures, posture, and tone of voice can all convey confidence, openness, and authority. For instance, maintaining an open posture and using purposeful gestures signals approachability and control, while a calm and steady tone of voice communicates confidence (Knapp & Hall, 2009). Together, these elements enhance your ability to connect, influence, and build trust with others.

By becoming more aware of how appearance, first impressions, and nonverbal communication intersect, you can navigate professional interactions more effectively, ensuring you project both confidence and authenticity. Moreover, acknowledging and respecting cultural differences in these areas can foster a more inclusive and respectful workplace environment (Hall, 1966).

Just as nonverbal cues communicate your professionalism, your attire is an extension of how you choose to present yourself in every interaction. Let's explore how selecting the right attire can help you reinforce your professional goals.

Choosing Attire Wisely

Understanding Your Audience

Selecting the right attire starts with understanding your audience and the environment you're entering. Different workplaces and professional settings have unique dress code expectations. Aligning your attire with these norms allows you to fit in while still protecting your personal brand of professionalism (Rafaeli & Pratt, 1993).

- **Corporate Settings**: In formal corporate environments, traditional business attire like suits, blazers, and dress shoes is the norm.

Opt for classic colors such as black, navy, and gray to convey authority and professionalism.

- **Creative Industries**: Creative fields offer more flexibility in personal expression. However, maintaining a polished look is key. Incorporate unique accessories or bold colors that complement your appearance without being distracting.
- **Casual Workplaces**: In more relaxed settings, business casual attire, such as dress pants, skirts, and smart-casual shoes, allows for comfort without sacrificing professionalism.

Your goal is to balance the expectations of the environment with your personal style, presenting yourself as both authentic and appropriate (Goffman, 1959).

Balancing Professionalism and Personal Style

Your attire should not only reflect professionalism but also convey your individuality. When you dress with confidence, you project your unique value while adhering to the professional standards of your environment (Dittmar, 2007).

- **Personal Touches**: Subtle accessories like a statement necklace, a watch, or a colorful scarf can infuse your personality into a polished look.
- **Timeless Staples**: Invest in versatile pieces such as a well-fitted blazer, tailored trousers, or a classic dress that can easily transition across professional settings.
- **Staying Current**: While professionalism is key, incorporating modern trends in a subtle way can refresh your look and keep you relevant in a fast-evolving world.

This balance allows you to project authority while staying true to who you are.

Fabric and Fit

The fabric and fit of your clothing play a significant role in how others perceive you. Quality fabrics and proper fit not only elevate your appearance but also help you stay comfortable and focused (Damhorst, 1990).

- **Opt for Quality**: Choose durable, breathable materials like cotton, wool, and silk. These fabrics offer comfort and a professional, polished look.
- **Tailor for Fit**: Well-fitting clothes can make all the difference. Avoid clothing that pulls or sags, and consider tailoring to ensure your outfit flatters your shape and presents a clean, professional appearance.
- **Functionality**: Your attire should suit the environment and season. Choose lightweight fabrics for warmer months and heavier ones for colder weather—ensuring comfort while maintaining professionalism.

By choosing the right fabric and fit, you project competence and confidence, allowing your work to take center stage.

Empowering Attire Choices

Your wardrobe choices should empower you, allowing your skills and contributions to be the focus rather than your attire. Thoughtful choices reflect confidence and professionalism, supporting your role in any environment (Entwistle, 2000).

- **Professional Styles**: Choose necklines and hemlines that balance style and professionalism. Aim for a look that commands attention for the right reasons.
- **Fit and Coverage**: Well-fitted clothing that offers appropriate coverage enhances your confidence, ensuring the focus remains on your capabilities.
- **Refined Accessories**: Choose subtle accessories that complement, rather than overpower, your outfit. This reinforces professionalism while showcasing your individuality.

Empowering attire choices align with your goals, projecting confidence and competence without distraction.

Navigating Dress Codes with Confidence

Mastering dress codes is about making strategic choices that align with professionalism while reflecting your personal style (Simmel, 1957). Here's how to navigate common dress codes:

- **Casual**: For laid-back settings like tech startups, opt for neat, presentable pieces like jeans, t-shirts, and casual shoes, ensuring you maintain a polished appearance.

- **Smart Casual**: Blend comfort with sophistication by wearing blazers, dress shirts, and neat jeans or trousers for informal meetings or networking events.

- **Business Casual**: A popular dress code, business casual balances formality and comfort with items like dress pants, skirts, and loafers for day-to-day office interactions.

- **Business Formal**: For high-level meetings and formal events, wear suits, ties, and formal dresses in classic colors like black and navy to showcase authority and professionalism.

- **Semi-Formal**: Ideal for evening events, choose cocktail dresses or tailored suits for a touch of elegance that maintains a professional edge.

- **Black Tie & White Tie**: Reserved for the most formal events, black tie requires tuxedos or evening gowns, while white tie is even more formal, calling for tailcoats and ball gowns.

Navigating dress codes with confidence means understanding expectations while interpreting them through your own lens of style and professionalism.

Interpreting Dress Codes with Confidence

Decoding dress codes allows you to step into any setting with certainty. Here's how to approach it:

- **Pay Attention to Invitations**: Invitations often provide valuable clues about the expected attire, helping you feel prepared and polished.

- **Consider the Venue**: The setting informs the formality. A corporate gala will require different attire than a casual networking event. Understanding the environment helps you make the right choices.

- **Ask When in Doubt**: If you're unsure about the dress code, don't hesitate to ask the host or organizer for clarification. It's better to be prepared than underdressed.

- **Lean Toward Formality**: When uncertain, it's better to overdress slightly than risk being too casual. A more formal look reflects respect for the event and those in attendance.

By mastering dress codes, you turn any event or professional setting into an opportunity to stand out with confidence and grace.

Maintaining Authenticity in Professional Attire

Balancing authenticity with professional dress codes allows you to present a polished yet genuine version of yourself in any environment (Entwistle, 2015). It's about making empowered choices that reflect both your individuality and professionalism.

- **Incorporate Personal Touches**: Add subtle, meaningful elements to your outfit that showcase your personality. A favorite scarf, statement necklace, or sleek watch can personalize your look without compromising professionalism. These small touches allow you to stay true to yourself while aligning with workplace expectations.

- **Prioritize Comfort and Confidence**: When you feel comfortable, your confidence naturally shines. Choose attire that adheres to the dress code but also empowers you. Confidence is your most valuable accessory, and it shows in how you carry yourself and interact with others.

- **Stay True to Your Style**: Adapting to professional environments doesn't mean losing your individuality. Choose clothing that reflects who you are while still respecting dress codes. Authenticity fosters deeper connections, making you more approachable and relatable. By staying true to your style, you reinforce your personal brand and project confidence.

Authenticity is key—not only does it help you meet professional expectations, but it also enhances your ability to connect with others and command respect.

Dress Code Adaptability: Navigating Professional Settings with Confidence

Being adaptable in your wardrobe empowers you to transition effortlessly between different professional settings, ensuring you always look polished and appropriate for any occasion.

- **Build a Versatile Wardrobe**: Invest in key staples that work across various dress codes. A classic blazer, for example, pairs just as well with jeans for a smart-casual look as it does with tailored pants for a more formal appearance. Versatile pieces offer flexibility and ease as you navigate different environments.

- **Master Layering**: Layering is a simple way to adjust your outfit's formality. Adding a structured blazer or cardigan can elevate a casual look, while removing a jacket or tie can instantly relax a formal outfit. Layers also help you adapt to changing climates or settings with ease.

- **Seasonal Adaptability**: Choose fabrics that suit the season without sacrificing professionalism. Lightweight materials like linen or cotton are perfect for warmer weather, while wool or tweed provide warmth and structure in colder months. Dressing appropriately for the season ensures comfort, confidence, and style.

- **Cultural Sensitivity**: In multicultural or international settings, being aware of cultural norms around attire is crucial. Dressing with cultural awareness shows respect and helps you navigate professional interactions with grace. It demonstrates adaptability and fosters stronger relationships in diverse environments.

Adapting to different dress codes not only shows professionalism but also highlights your ability to be versatile and prepared for any professional situation.

Understanding Appearance and Perception: The Role of Cultural Sensitivity

In today's interconnected world, understanding appearance and perception is not just about personal presentation; it also involves recognizing the cultural nuances that influence how individuals are perceived based on their appearance (Hall, 1966). Cultural sensitivity plays a crucial role in this dynamic, as it acknowledges the diverse backgrounds and experiences that shape how individuals interact with one another in professional settings.

1. Cultural Variations in Appearance Standards:

Cultural backgrounds heavily influence what is considered appropriate or professional attire. Different cultures have distinct norms regarding clothing, grooming, and even body language. For example:

- In some cultures, traditional clothing is a source of pride and identity, and wearing such attire in the workplace can be an expression of cultural heritage. However, this may not always be understood or appreciated by colleagues from different backgrounds.

- Hair styles, makeup, and body modifications (such as tattoos or piercings) can carry varying significance across cultures. What one culture views as a form of self-expression may be perceived differently in another, leading to misunderstandings or bias.

2. Perception of Professionalism:

The standards of professionalism can vary widely based on cultural norms. Individuals from non-Western cultures, for instance, might face challenges in environments where Western standards dominate. These challenges can include:

- **Implicit Bias:** Colleagues may unconsciously associate certain appearances with stereotypes, impacting professional opportunities, hiring decisions, or promotions. For example, individuals with natural hairstyles might face bias in environments that favor straight hair.

- **Microaggressions:** Subtle, often unintentional comments or actions can reinforce stereotypes about appearance. For example, comments questioning a person's capabilities based on their attire or hair can undermine their confidence and professional presence.

3. Intersectionality and Additional Challenges:

Understanding appearance and perception also involves recognizing the intersectionality of race, gender, and socioeconomic status. For instance:

- Women of color may experience compounded challenges regarding how they are perceived based on both their gender and racial background. They may navigate expectations that differ significantly from those of their white counterparts.

- Socioeconomic background can also affect appearance and access to professional attire, creating disparities in how individuals are perceived in the workplace. Those who may not have the financial means to invest in a "professional wardrobe" can face unfair judgments.

4. The Importance of Cultural Sensitivity:

Cultural sensitivity is essential for creating inclusive workplaces where all individuals feel valued and respected. Here's how it can be fostered:

- **Education and Awareness:** Organizations can provide training on cultural competence to help employees understand the diverse backgrounds of their colleagues. This education can lead to greater empathy and reduced bias in perceptions of appearance.

- **Encouraging Diversity:** Promoting diversity in leadership and decision-making can help ensure that a variety of cultural perspectives are considered when establishing workplace norms regarding appearance.

- **Open Dialogue:** Encouraging conversations about cultural differences and perceptions can help dispel misconceptions. Creating safe spaces for discussions about appearance allows individuals to share their experiences and challenges openly.

Adapting to dress codes in different professional settings is just one layer of the puzzle. In our increasingly interconnected world, cultural sensitivity plays an equally important role in how we manage our appearance.

Conclusion

Recognizing the interplay between appearance, perception, and cultural sensitivity is vital for fostering an inclusive environment where everyone can thrive (Crane, 2012). By understanding the unique challenges faced by individuals from diverse backgrounds, organizations and colleagues can work together to create a culture of respect and appreciation for all. This awareness empowers individuals to navigate their professional lives with confidence, knowing that their appearance is celebrated rather than judged.

As we conclude our exploration of the **Power of Perception**, it's clear that how we present ourselves and how others perceive us can significantly influence our professional experiences and interactions. We've examined the importance of understanding cultural sensitivity and the diverse challenges faced by individuals from various backgrounds. Recognizing that appearance is not merely about aesthetics but also about conveying confidence, professionalism, and authenticity is vital for navigating today's complex workplace.

Throughout this chapter, we've discussed practical strategies for managing perceptions, such as honing your appearance to align with your professional goals, utilizing non-verbal cues effectively, and embracing the unique aspects of your identity. By owning your appearance and how you're perceived, you hold the power to shape your professional journey and command respect wherever you go.

Now that we've explored how appearance and perception can shape your professional journey, it's time to reflect on where you stand. The following assessment will help you gauge your current awareness and highlight areas for growth, giving you actionable steps to enhance your professional presence.

UNDERSTANDING APPEARANCE AND PERCEPTION

Assessment: Appearance and Perception Awareness Scale

Instructions: Rate each statement on a scale from 1 (Strongly disagree) to 5 (Strongly agree).

1. I understand how my appearance affects others' perceptions of me.
2. I feel confident in presenting myself professionally.
3. I can adapt my appearance to different professional settings.
4. I am aware of the impact of non-verbal cues on perception.
5. I can use my appearance to convey confidence and competence.
6. I pay attention to my grooming and attire.
7. I understand the dress code expectations in my industry.
8. I can adjust my appearance based on the context (e.g., formal meetings vs. casual events).
9. I am aware of how my body language affects others' perceptions.
10. I feel comfortable expressing my personal style within professional boundaries.

Understanding Appearance and Perception

Scoring Interpretation

- 10-20: Low Awareness of Appearance and Perception

Description: Individuals in this range may have limited understanding of how their appearance affects others' perceptions. They might struggle to present themselves professionally and be unaware of the impact of non-verbal cues.

Action Steps:

1. Seek Feedback: Ask for feedback on your professional appearance from trusted colleagues.

2. Experiment with Styles: Try different styles to find what works best for you in professional settings.

3. Learn About Non-Verbal Communication: Educate yourself on the impact of non-verbal cues on perception.

- 21-35: Moderate Awareness of Appearance and Perception

Description: Individuals in this range have a moderate understanding of how their appearance affects others' perceptions. They can present themselves professionally in most situations but may still experience occasional uncertainty.

Action Steps:

1. Observe Others: Watch how others in your field present themselves and learn from their behavior.

2. Refine Non-Verbal Skills: Practice and refine your non-verbal communication skills.

3. Reflect on Past Experiences: Think about past situations where your appearance influenced others' perceptions and what you can learn from them.

- 36-50: High Awareness of Appearance and Perception

Description: Individuals in this range have a strong understanding of how their appearance affects others' perceptions. They can present themselves confidently and professionally and are aware of the impact of non-verbal cues.

Action Steps:

1. Continue Presenting Confidently: Maintain your ability to present yourself professionally.

2. Share Tips: Help others improve their professional appearance and non-verbal communication skills.

3. Reflect on Successes: Regularly reflect on your experiences and celebrate your effective use of appearance and perception.

As we wrap up Chapter 7, it's evident that managing appearance and perception goes far beyond surface-level decisions about attire. It's about navigating the subtle and powerful dynamics of how we're seen, while embracing our authenticity and understanding the cultural contexts that shape professional environments. Through this chapter, you've explored how perception can be your ally or your challenge in advancing your career.

Now, take the opportunity to reflect on what you've learned through the assessment. It will help you gauge your current approach and highlight areas for growth as you continue building your professional presence. In the next chapter, we'll shift focus to another crucial aspect of professional success—navigating difficult conversations and asserting your voice when it matters most. Let's continue the journey toward empowerment and confidence in every interaction.

You've just gained valuable insights into the power of perception and how your appearance plays a role in shaping professional interactions. By understanding the nuances of appearance, attire, and cultural sensitivity, you're now better equipped to project the image you want and control how others perceive you.

Next, we'll take a step outside the office and explore how to navigate after-hours events with grace and professionalism. In **Chapter 8**, we'll dive into **after-hours etiquette**, where we'll discuss maintaining boundaries and professionalism even in informal settings.

CHAPTER

08

AFTER-HOURS ETIQUETTE: NAVIGATING PROFESSIONAL INTERACTIONS BEYOND THE OFFICE

"The Hilltop Encounter: Navigating Unwanted Advances"

The Unwanted Advance

I was working as an assistant to a boss I deeply admired. Our professional relationship was sprinkled with light-hearted moments, often shared over lunch. I was young and carefree, and my friendly demeanor seemed harmless. My boss was a charismatic leader, someone who had taken me under his wing and mentored me through the early stages of my career. I looked up to him, not just as a superior, but as a role model.

One evening, after a particularly productive dinner meeting, he offered to drive me back to the office. As we drove, the conversation flowed easily, filled with laughter and anecdotes from the day. However, as we approached a secluded hill, I felt a twinge of confusion. I asked where we were going, but he just smiled and parked the car, turning off the engine. The silence that followed was heavy with unspoken tension.

Without warning, he leaned in to kiss me. I was taken aback. This was my boss, someone I respected and trusted. My mind raced as I tried to process what was happening. In an attempt to diffuse the situation, I laughed it off, told him I wasn't interested, and asked to go back to the office. In my youthful naivety, I even considered it a compliment, a misguided attempt to rationalize the inappropriate advance.

But deep down, I knew it was wrong. His actions were unprofessional and crossed a boundary that should never have been breached. This experience was a harsh lesson in the importance of maintaining professional boundaries, regardless of how friendly a relationship might seem. It also highlighted the need to recognize and address inappropriate behavior, no matter the source.

Just as I had to learn the hard way about setting clear boundaries, the rise of digital communication tools has introduced a new challenge for professionals. Navigating after-hours communication can blur lines between personal and professional, making it even more crucial to maintain boundaries in the digital age.

Navigating Late-Night Communication

The advent of technology has significantly transformed modern workplace culture, blurring the lines between professional and personal time. With the proliferation of smartphones, laptops, and instant messaging apps, communication often spills over into after-hours, creating a new dynamic in how we interact with colleagues and manage work-life balance (Derks et al., 2014).

Shift in Workplace Culture

The boundaries between work and personal time have evolved, largely due to the rise of digital communication tools. What was once a clear distinction between office hours and personal time has blurred, making employees more accessible beyond traditional working hours (Mazmanian et al., 2013). This shift impacts industries across the board and is driven by several key factors:

- **Globalization:** As companies expand across borders, teams are spread over multiple time zones, often requiring communication outside typical business hours to keep projects moving efficiently.

- **Remote Work:** The rise of remote work, accelerated by the COVID-19 pandemic, has redefined the work-life balance. Working from home has made it harder for many to fully disconnect, resulting in more frequent after-hours communication.

- **Expectations for Quick Responses:** The ease and speed of communication via instant messaging and email have created an expectation for immediate replies. This constant accessibility can lead to pressure to always be "on," even during personal time.

- **Project Urgency and Tight Deadlines:** In fast-paced industries, the need for immediate action on urgent projects or deadlines often requires after-hours communication to keep things on track.

This shift in workplace culture affects all industries, and the 2 AM Code is your constant guide. Whether you're working in tech, finance, or healthcare, upholding your boundaries and dignity—even in the face of urgent deadlines—remains the core of maintaining professional integrity, no matter the industry.

Common Scenarios Across Industries

After-hours communication is prevalent across many industries, each presenting unique challenges and expectations. Here's a look at how this plays out in different sectors:

- **Technology and IT:** In the tech world, where tight deadlines and continuous project updates are the norm, after-hours communication is often necessary to address urgent issues and keep operations running smoothly (Greenbaum, 2019).

- **Finance and Consulting:** Professionals in these sectors frequently manage clients across multiple time zones, making late-night calls and emails common to meet client needs and deadlines (Fleming, 2015).

- **Healthcare:** Administrative and managerial roles in healthcare require after-hours coordination to ensure patient care, manage emergencies, and maintain operational efficiency (Schneider, 2016).

- **Media and Entertainment:** This industry, where events and productions occur at all hours, relies heavily on after-hours communication to ensure timely updates and effective coordination.

In each of these industries, the need for after-hours communication is undeniable. Yet, the **2 AM Code** empowers you to maintain your professional boundaries, no matter the time. It reminds you that even in late-night scenarios, you are in full control of your space, dignity, and professionalism.

While after-hours communication is necessary in many industries, it also brings with it the risk of miscommunication or inappropriate interactions if not handled with care. Let's explore how to maintain professionalism during these times."

Potential for Misunderstanding or Inappropriate Interactions

Late-night communications can easily be misinterpreted due to their timing, which often feels more informal (Turel et al., 2011). To maintain professionalism, it's important to consider the following:

- **Tone and Clarity:** Messages sent late at night might be perceived as either overly casual or unnecessarily urgent. To avoid misinterpretation, be intentional with your language. Ensure your message is clear and concise.

  For instance, a casual tone in a late-night text might come across as overly familiar or even unprofessional. A simple shift in language—like using a formal greeting and avoiding abbreviations—can prevent misunderstandings.

- **Boundaries:** Late-night communication can blur the line between professional and personal life. It's crucial to respect boundaries to avoid causing discomfort or creating inappropriate situations.

Beyond simply ensuring clarity, the 2 AM Code reminds us that professionalism extends to every interaction, no matter the time of day. Maintaining a respectful tone—whether in person or via a late-night text—upholds your values and preserves your professional re-lationships.

Professional Tone

Maintaining a professional tone is crucial, even in more informal set-tings or during after-hours communication. Here are key ways to en-sure professionalism:

- **Using Full Names or Titles:** Addressing colleagues and supervi-sors by their full names or titles demonstrates respect and pro-fessionalism. For example, "Dear Dr. Smith" maintains a respect-ful tone, whereas "Hey John" may come across as too casual, especially in a professional context (Goffman, 1959).

- **Polite Language:** Opt for polite and considerate phrasing. In-stead of saying, "Check this out," reframe it as, "Could you please review this document?" This helps to keep the tone formal and respectful, even in after-hours communication.

Timing Considerations

The appropriateness of after-hours communication largely depends on company culture and the urgency of the issue at hand:

- **Company Culture:** Each company has its own expectations re-garding after-hours availability. While some workplaces have flexible schedules, others may adhere strictly to a 9-to-5 frame-work. Before sending late-night messages, familiarize yourself with your company's norms to avoid misalignment.

- **Urgency:** Limit after-hours messages to urgent matters that truly cannot wait until the next business day. For example, a critical system failure warrants immediate communication, whereas a routine update can be postponed. Evaluating the urgency be-fore hitting send ensures you respect both your colleagues' time and professional boundaries.

Not only is it important to send messages at the right time, but setting expectations around when a response is needed also plays a key role in respecting boundaries (Derks et al., 2014).

Response Expectations

Setting and Communicating Boundaries clear communication of your availability is essential for maintaining work-life balance. Let colleagues know your specific work hours and when they can expect a response. For instance, 'I am available for work-related discussions from 9 AM to 6 PM, and I'll respond to urgent matters only after 6 PM.' Additionally, encourage team discussions to establish mutually agreed-upon response times, such as a 24-hour window for non-urgent matters (Mazmanian et al., 2013).

To ensure after-hours communication remains efficient and respectful, it's important to strategize how and when you send messages. Setting response expectations isn't just about managing time; it's about honoring the 2 AM Code, which empowers you to control your space while still being an effective communicator. Let's look at effective strategies for managing these communications.

Strategies for Effective Communication: Setting Parameters and Planning Ahead

Effective communication requires not only clarity but also thoughtful planning (Greenbaum, 2019). Here's how to strategically manage your after-hours communications while respecting professional boundaries:

- **Schedule Communications Strategically:** Instead of sending texts or emails late at night, use scheduling tools to delay your messages until regular business hours. This approach respects your colleagues' personal time and avoids creating an expectation for immediate responses. For example, if you draft an email at 10 PM, schedule it to be sent at 8 AM the following morning. This ensures your message is received at an appropriate time, promoting healthier communication habits.

- **Utilize Out-of-Office Replies:** Out-of-office messages aren't just for vacations; they are effective for managing short-term unavailability as well. Whether you're in back-to-back meetings or need focused work time, an out-of-office reply can inform colleagues of your temporary unavailability. For example, "I'm unavailable until 3 PM but will respond to your message after that time" helps manage expectations and reduces the pressure to respond instantly.

Defining Acceptable After-Hours Communication Boundaries

Maintaining a healthy work-life balance requires clear communication boundaries that distinguish personal and professional time:

- **Boundaries: Personal vs. Professional:** It's vital to separate work from personal communication to maintain balance. Keep personal messages casual, while work-related communications should remain professional—even after hours. For example, it's appropriate to discuss weekend plans informally, but professional discussions—such as project updates—should be reserved for regular working hours.

- **Acceptable Topics:** During off-hours, limit conversations to urgent work matters. While non-work-related chats can be appropriate, avoid discussing sensitive or confidential topics outside of work hours. A good guideline is: casual social talk is fine, but professional, confidential matters should wait until business hours to avoid miscommunication or unintended pressure.

Defining personal communication boundaries is only one part of the equation. Establishing clear guidelines for after-hours communication across your team or organization ensures everyone is on the same page.

Establishing Guidelines for After-Hours Communication

Creating a clear framework for after-hours communication helps manage expectations and ensures professionalism, even when working outside regular hours.

- **Framework for Guidelines:** Set specific boundaries for when after-hours communication is appropriate and what qualifies as urgent. This includes determining acceptable hours for contact and emphasizing the importance of prioritizing urgency. For instance, "After 8 PM, only urgent matters should be communicated, while non-urgent issues can be addressed during the next business day." This framework keeps work from encroaching on personal time and ensures that communication stays respectful of boundaries.

Who to Contact in Different Situations

Understanding who to reach out to in various scenarios is key to maintaining efficient communication without disrupting others unnecessarily.

- **Emergency Contacts:** Designate specific people for emergency situations to streamline urgent communications. For example, "In case of a critical system failure, contact your direct manager or the IT support team." This ensures that emergencies are handled swiftly while keeping communication channels focused and effective.

- **Non-Emergency Contacts:** Set clear expectations for who should not be contacted after hours unless it's absolutely necessary. For example, "Avoid reaching out to colleagues outside of your immediate team for non-urgent matters after hours." This reinforces boundaries and respects others' time, helping maintain a healthy balance between urgency and non-essential matters.

Types of Communication

When defining after-hours communication boundaries, it's important to differentiate between urgent matters that require immediate attention and non-urgent updates that can wait until the next business day. Establish clear response expectations to reduce pressure and maintain balance. For example, "For urgent matters, a response within one hour is expected, while non-urgent items can be addressed the following business day.

Knowing who to contact is just one part of the process. Clear response time expectations are equally important to ensure efficient communication without overburdening anyone after hours.

Setting Response Time Expectations

Establishing clear response time expectations for after-hours communication is essential for maintaining efficiency and reducing stress across teams (Turel et al., 2011).

- **Agree on Response Times:** Define and agree upon response times based on the urgency of the communication. This ensures clarity and reduces anxiety about when responses are needed. For instance, "For urgent matters, a response within one hour is expected, while non-urgent emails can be addressed within 24 hours." This helps both senders and receivers know when they can expect a reply and whether immediate action is necessary.

- **Set Availability Boundaries:** Communicate specific times when you will not be available to respond, ensuring colleagues know when to expect a follow-up. For example, "I will not be available after 8 PM, but I will respond to any messages first thing in the morning." Setting these boundaries fosters a healthy work-life balance while keeping communication transparent and manageable.

Boundary-Setting Scripts for After-Hours Communication

Setting clear boundaries with colleagues and supervisors ensures mutual respect. Here are examples of how to communicate your availability across different platforms:

- *Text Message:* 'Hi [Colleague's Name], I usually avoid work-related texts after 8 PM to spend time with my family. If it's urgent, feel free to call me; otherwise, I'll get back to you first thing in the morning.'

- *Email:* 'Dear [Colleague's Name], I typically check emails until 6 PM. If an email comes in after that time, I'll respond the next business day unless it's urgent.'

- *Supervisor Conversation:* 'Hi [Supervisor's Name], I try to disconnect after 8 PM to maintain work-life balance. I'll address urgent matters promptly, but non-urgent tasks will be handled the next day.'"

Communicating boundaries thoughtfully sets expectations and promotes mutual respect, helping both you and your colleagues or supervisors maintain a healthy and productive working relationship.

Setting clear boundaries is the first step, but fostering an environment of mutual respect around those boundaries ensures they're upheld by both you and your colleagues.

Fostering Mutual Respect through Boundary Communication

Establishing boundaries is not only about protecting your time, but also about cultivating a culture of mutual respect in the workplace (Schneider, 2016). Clear, respectful communication encourages others to do the same, creating an environment where balance and well-being are prioritized. Here are key elements to emphasize:

Respect for Others' Boundaries:

Just as you expect your boundaries to be respected, extend the same courtesy to your colleagues. If a colleague has shared that they are unavailable after certain hours, honor that unless it's a true emergency. Mutual respect for boundaries ensures that everyone can enjoy a healthier balance between work and personal life.

Maintaining a Healthy Work-Life Balance:

Respecting boundaries isn't just beneficial to the individual—it supports a more productive and harmonious workplace. When employees maintain a clear separation between work and personal time, it leads to increased focus during working hours, greater overall productivity, and improved well-being.

Encouraging Open Communication:

Honest communication about availability and expectations is key. Being upfront with your colleagues and supervisors fosters transparency, helping to prevent misunderstandings and ensuring everyone is aligned. Clear communication ensures that boundaries aren't just set—they're respected.

Understanding the Risks of Constant Availability

In today's hyper-connected world, the expectation to be "always-on" is becoming increasingly common (Derks et al., 2014). While digital communication tools and remote work offer flexibility, they also come with significant risks if boundaries aren't established.

Burnout and Productivity Decline:

Constant availability can lead to burnout, characterized by chronic exhaustion and a diminished sense of accomplishment. The American Psychological Association reports that 79% of employees experience work-related stress, with many noting the toll it takes on their mental health. Frequent interruptions during off-hours also harm productivity, making it harder to concentrate and complete tasks efficiently.

Heightened Stress Levels:

The pressure to be accessible at all times can take a serious toll on mental health. Studies show that this constant connectivity can lead to anxiety, difficulty focusing, and, ultimately, job dissatisfaction. When employees feel overwhelmed, their engagement and satisfaction with work diminish, leading to higher turnover rates.

Blurring the Lines Between Work and Personal Life:

Being perpetually on-call makes it difficult to fully disengage from work, which can negatively affect personal relationships and overall well-being. The inability to switch off from work can lead to a sense of being "always at work," which exacerbates stress and contributes to work-family conflict. This blurred boundary not only reduces the quality of personal time but can also lead to resentment toward work.

Given the risks of constant availability, organizations have a critical role in either exacerbating or alleviating these pressures by creating environments that support work-life balance.

The Role of Organizations in Promoting Healthier Boundaries

Employers have the power to either perpetuate the "always-on" culture or help dismantle it by fostering a work environment that respects employees' personal time. Encouraging healthy boundaries and promoting policies that protect off-hours can greatly reduce burnout and boost productivity in the long run (Mazmanian et al., 2013).

Implementing Healthy Policies:

Workplaces that create clear expectations about after-hours availability and respect personal time see greater employee satisfaction and reduced turnover. By advocating for boundaries, such as limiting after-hours emails or enforcing no-work weekends, companies send a clear message that work-life balance is a priority.

By recognizing the negative consequences of constant availability and supporting a culture that values time off, both individuals and organizations can achieve a more balanced and sustainable work environment. When you understand the risks of the "always-on" mentality, you're empowered to take control of your availability, maintaining your well-being and thriving both personally and professionally.

Fostering a Culture of Work-Life Balance

Establishing and maintaining clear boundaries not only enhances individual well-being but also cultivates a healthier, more productive workplace culture. To support this balance, advocate for policies like a "no emails after 7 PM" rule or designating weekends as work-free zones. Leading by example and encouraging your team to adopt similar boundaries creates an environment where personal time is respected, leading to greater overall productivity and employee satisfaction.

While fostering a culture of work-life balance at the organizational level is essential, the 2 AM Code reminds us that it starts with personal accountability. Setting your own boundaries—whether it's when to respond to emails or when to disconnect—reinforces the principle that you control your time, maintaining your dignity in the process.

Setting Personal Boundaries

Start by deciding specific times when you'll be available for work-related communications and when you'll prioritize personal time. Clearly communicating these boundaries helps others understand your off-duty times, which supports a balanced integration of work and personal life.

Creating Cultural Norms in the Workplace

Fostering a culture that respects boundaries at the organizational level is key to promoting long-term balance and productivity. This could involve establishing company-wide norms, such as limiting after-hours emails or implementing a "no-work weekends" policy. When these boundaries are embraced across the workplace, employees feel empowered to thrive both professionally and personally, contributing to a more sustainable and harmonious work culture.

Advocating for Policies that Support Boundaries

To truly promote a healthy work-life balance, workplace policies need to reinforce clear boundaries. Here are practical strategies to advocate for within your organization:

No Emails After 7 PM:

Encourage a policy where non-urgent emails are not sent after 7 PM. This provides employees the opportunity to disconnect, recharge, and return to work feeling refreshed. By enforcing this policy, the workplace respects personal time, reducing stress and enhancing productivity during work hours.

No-Work Weekends:

Advocate for a culture where weekends are strictly reserved for personal time, with minimal work-related communication. This ensures that employees have a clear separation between work and personal life, leading to improved mental health and job satisfaction.

Flexible Work Arrangements:

Support policies that allow for flexible working hours, giving employees the ability to manage both work and personal responsibilities effectively. Flexibility empowers employees to maintain a balance that works for their individual needs, improving overall engagement and reducing burnout.

Strategies for Maintaining Availability Expectations

To reduce stress and foster clear communication, it's essential to set and maintain expectations around availability. Here's how to make this happen:

Communicate Work Hours:

Be proactive in communicating your availability to colleagues and supervisors. For instance, you can let them know, "I am available for work discussions from 9 AM to 6 PM. After 6 PM, I will only respond to urgent matters." This clarity ensures that everyone knows when you are reachable and when you need personal time.

Set Availability Status:

Use digital tools to indicate when you're unavailable, such as setting email auto-responders or updating your messaging app status. For example, "Out of office until 9 AM tomorrow. I will respond to your message then." This helps colleagues manage their expectations and reduces the pressure to respond immediately.

Discuss and Align Expectations:

Have open discussions with your team about response time expectations, especially for after-hours communication. Agree on what constitutes an urgent matter and set reasonable expectations for how quickly responses are needed. This approach reduces the stress of feeling constantly on-call while ensuring that critical issues are addressed promptly.

By creating and communicating clear boundaries, you empower yourself to maintain a healthier work-life balance. At the same time, advocating for these policies within your workplace helps to create a culture that values well-being and respects personal time—leading to better overall productivity and employee satisfaction.

Mindfulness and Self-Care Strategies

To maintain a healthy balance between work and personal life, it's essential to build regular breaks and digital detox periods into your routine. Schedule personal time into your calendar, and treat it as non-negotiable. Take a few moments each day to engage in mindful breathing exercises or meditate to reduce stress. Prioritizing physical activity, hobbies, and sleep also plays a crucial role in preventing burnout and ensuring you return to work feeling refreshed.

Disconnection Tactics for Preserving Personal Time

Taking deliberate steps to disconnect from work allows you to maintain the boundaries necessary for a balanced life:

Digital Detox Periods:

Schedule regular periods where you disconnect from all electronic devices. Whether it's a few hours in the evening or an entire day on the weekend, these breaks from digital communication help you recharge without distractions.

Blocking Time Off in Calendars:

Reserve blocks of personal time in your calendar just as you would schedule meetings. Treat this time as non-negotiable, ensuring you have moments to relax and rejuvenate.

Setting Boundaries:

Communicate clear boundaries with colleagues and supervisors regarding your availability. For instance, "I am available for work discussions from 9 AM to 6 PM. After 6 PM, I will respond only to urgent matters." This prevents unnecessary interruptions and ensures others respect your personal time.

Navigating after-hours interactions is a vital skill in today's professional world, where the lines between work and personal life often blur (Greenbaum, 2019). Throughout this chapter, we've explored the intricacies of after-hours etiquette—from managing social gatherings to effectively handling after-hours communication.

As you reflect on the lessons in this chapter, consider how your current boundaries and communication habits align with these principles. How do you balance your professional obligations with your personal time? Are there areas where you can adjust to create a healthier, more empowered balance?

The following assessment will help you evaluate your current practices and reveal areas for improvement. By aligning your habits with these guidelines, you can enhance your professional relationships while maintaining the boundaries that support your overall well-being.

ASSESSMENT: AFTER-HOURS COMMUNICATION COMFORT SCALE

Instructions: Rate each statement on a scale from 1 (Strongly disagree) to 5 (Strongly agree).

1. I feel comfortable engaging in work-related conversations after hours.
2. I can maintain professional boundaries in social settings.
3. I know how to navigate informal work gatherings.
4. I can switch between professional and casual communication styles.
5. I feel confident in my ability to handle after-hours interactions.
6. I can engage in small talk with colleagues.
7. I am aware of the appropriate topics for after-hours discussions.
8. I can manage my time effectively during social events.
9. I can maintain a professional image even in casual settings.
10. I can handle conflicts that arise during after-hours interactions.

Scoring Interpretation

- 10-20: Low Comfort with After-Hours Communication

Description: Individuals in this range may feel uncomfortable engaging in work-related conversations after hours. They might struggle to maintain professional boundaries in social settings and find it challenging to switch between professional and casual communication styles.

Action Steps:

1. Set Clear Boundaries: Define your boundaries for after-hours communication and stick to them.

2. Practice Casual Conversations: Engage in casual conversations in a safe environment to build comfort.

3. Observe Others: Watch how others navigate after-hours interactions and learn from their behavior.

- 21-35: Moderate Comfort with After-Hours Communication

Description: Individuals in this range are moderately comfortable with after-hours communication. They can engage in work-related conversations and maintain professional boundaries in most social settings but may still experience occasional discomfort.

Action Steps:

1. Attend Informal Work Events: Participate in more informal work events to build confidence.

2. Reflect on Past Interactions: Think about past after-hours interactions and what you can learn from them.

3. Balance Professional and Casual Communication: Practice switching between professional and casual communication styles.

- 36-50: High Comfort with After-Hours Communication

Description: Individuals in this range are highly comfortable with after-hours communication. They can engage in work-related conversations, maintain professional boundaries, and switch between professional and casual communication styles with ease.

Action Steps:

1. Continue Balancing Communication Styles: Maintain your ability to switch between professional and casual communication styles.

2. Offer Tips to Colleagues: Share your strategies for managing after-hours dynamics with colleagues.

3. Reflect on Successes: Regularly reflect on your after-hours interactions and celebrate your successes.

You've mastered the essential skills for navigating after-hours professional interactions, ensuring that you maintain your reputation and professionalism even in informal settings. Whether it's a work dinner or a casual networking event, you now have the tools to navigate these spaces with confidence.

As we move forward, it's time to focus on advocating for yourself in one of the most important aspects of your career—**salary negoti- ation**. In **Chapter 9**, you'll discover how to champion your worth and negotiate effectively for the compensation you deserve.

09

CHAMPIONING YOUR WORTH: STRATEGIES FOR EFFECTIVE SALARY NEGOTIATION

I landed a high-paying job as the right-hand person to a boss who was schizophrenic and had manic depression. The role was both demanding and unpredictable, requiring me to navigate volatile relationships and manage the daily chaos. The job frequently involved alcohol indulgence, adding another layer of complexity. Despite the turmoil, I made more money than ever before, but I quickly learned that not all money is good money. Peace of mind is far more valuable than money earned in conflict.

One day, while driving with the Executive Director, a man who held significant power within the organization, he turned to me with a jarring question. He asked if I thought my female body parts were "golden" and why I wouldn't "give it up." I laughed it off as I often did, trying to maintain professionalism. But the question lingered, a stark reminder of the toxic environment I was in.

When I shared the incident with my male colleagues, they dismissed it as an offhand remark. Their reaction was disheartening, but it reinforced my resolve. His frustration stemmed from my refusal to compromise my integrity. Despite the pressure and inappropriate advances, I stood firm. My self-respect was not for sale. Yes, my lady parts are golden.

Reflecting on that time, I realized that true success is not measured solely by financial gain, but by the peace and integrity with which one earns it. Knowing your worth goes beyond tolerating toxic environments for a paycheck—it means advocating for yourself in every aspect of your professional life, especially during salary negotiations, where your value must be fully recognized.

Advocating for Yourself: Salary Negotiation

Understanding your worth is the foundation of any successful salary negotiation. Once you have a clear sense of your value, ground that understanding in concrete data. This means researching industry standards to ensure your expectations align with the current market (Babcock & Laschever, 2003). Explore salary surveys, industry reports, and platforms like Glassdoor and Payscale to gather comprehensive salary ranges for similar positions. Here's how to research effectively and bolster your negotiation strategy.

Incorporating Leadership Theories into Negotiation

Leadership theories can offer valuable frameworks for navigating salary negotiations. By applying these approaches, you enhance your communication, persuasion, and collaboration abilities (Yukl, 2013).

Transformational Leadership in Salary Negotiation

Transformational leadership is all about inspiring others and working toward a shared vision. In salary negotiations, this approach can help you frame the conversation in a way that fosters collaboration rather than conflict (Bass, 1985). Here's how it can empower you:

1. **Inspiring Collaboration**: Just as transformational leaders unite their teams, you can create a sense of partnership during the negotiation. Instead of viewing it as a confrontation, you can articulate how both you and the company can benefit from your compensation reflecting your value.

- □ **As an illustration**: "By aligning my salary with the contributions I bring to the team, we can ensure I remain fully committed to driving future success together."

2. **Building Trust and Rapport**: Trust is essential in any negotiation. By focusing on maintaining a positive relationship, you can foster an environment where both parties feel respected. When people feel valued, they're more open to compromise.

   - □ **Example**: "I value the work I've done here and the trust we've built. I'm confident we can find a solution that reflects my contributions and aligns with the company's goals."

3. **Encouraging Creative Solutions**: Transformational leaders are known for innovation. Similarly, you can introduce creative solutions in negotiations, such as proposing performance-based incentives or flexible benefits if the salary isn't fully negotiable.

   - □ **For Example**: "If budget limitations are a concern, we could explore performance-based incentives that reward my contributions to upcoming projects.

Situational Leadership in Salary Negotiation

Situational leadership is about being flexible and adjusting your approach depending on the context and people you're dealing with (Hersey & Blanchard, 1969). In salary negotiations, this adaptability helps you navigate different situations more effectively. Here's how it applies:

1. **Adapting Your Approach**: Just as situational leaders change their style based on the situation, you should adjust your negotiation strategy depending on the circumstances. In high-stakes situations, you may need to be more direct and assertive, but in discussions with multiple decision-makers, a more collaborative approach might be better.

   - □ **Example**: "In a high-stakes meeting where I know the decision is crucial, I'll emphasize my key achievements directly. But when working with a group, I'll aim for consensus, presenting how my value benefits the team as a whole."

2. **Assessing Readiness**: Effective negotiators, like situational leaders, understand the readiness and perspective of the other party. Gauge how prepared or open the employer is for negotiation—knowing this helps you tailor your arguments and communication style to better address their concerns and get to a resolution.

   □ **Example**: "I can sense if the employer is hesitant or facing budget constraints, so I'll adjust by offering flexible solutions like phased salary increases or other benefits."

3. **Empowering Others**: Situational leadership thrives on empowering others, and in a negotiation, it's about giving space for dialogue. You can encourage decision-makers to voice their perspectives and involve them in finding solutions, making the negotiation feel like a shared process.

   □ **Example**: "By asking questions about the company's goals and listening carefully, I can propose a salary package that meets their needs while still advocating for my worth.

Incorporating leadership theories such as transformational and situational leadership into your negotiation strategy not only enhances your effectiveness as a negotiator but also fosters a more collaborative and productive environment. By understanding these frameworks, you can adapt your approach based on the context and the individuals involved, ultimately leading to successful negotiations that benefit all parties.

Understanding Your Value:

Knowing your worth is just the beginning. To effectively negotiate your salary, you need to understand and articulate your value (Kolb, 2016). This involves a thorough self-assessment of your skills, experiences, and accomplishments.

Conducting a Self-Assessment: A Path to Empowering Your Negotiation

Before entering any negotiation, it's essential to have a clear understanding of your professional worth. The first step in championing your value is conducting a thorough self-assessment. This process not only boosts your confidence but also provides the concrete evidence you need to advocate for yourself effectively.

1. Compile a List of Achievements

To start, take time to reflect on your career journey and accomplishments. Here's how to frame it:

- **Skills**: Write down all the skills you've acquired—both technical abilities and interpersonal ones. Highlight your **hard skills**, like project management, coding, or data analysis, and your **soft skills**, such as leadership, communication, and problem-solving. Remember, both are equally valuable in shaping your career success.

- **Experiences**: Document the roles and responsibilities that have contributed to your growth. Reflect on key projects, leadership roles, and moments where you've stepped up to make an impact.

- **Accomplishments**: Be specific about your contributions. What are the significant milestones you've achieved? Whether it's leading a project that increased revenue, launching a successful marketing campaign, or streamlining operations, note down the **outcomes** and your **role** in making them happen. Focus on measurable results, as they provide strong talking points in negotiations.

2. Highlight Certifications and Unique Contributions

Your professional growth isn't just about day-to-day tasks. It's also about the extra steps you've taken to improve your skills and create value in unique ways.

- **Certifications**: Have you earned any certifications or completed training programs that set you apart? Whether it's technical certifications, leadership programs, or even industry-specific courses, these credentials enhance your marketability. They demonstrate your commitment to growth and development.

- **Unique Contributions**: Think about those moments where you went beyond the norm. Maybe you implemented a process that saved the company time, solved a persistent problem, or introduced an innovative solution. These contributions reflect your ability to think creatively and make a meaningful impact. Highlight them as part of your unique value.

3. Articulating Your Value: Connecting the Dots

Now that you've compiled your achievements and contributions, it's time to connect them to your value proposition. This is where the empowerment piece comes in. You're not just listing what you've done—you're translating that into the **value** you bring to any role.

- **Contribution to Company Success**: Be prepared to articulate exactly how your skills and experiences have driven success for your employers. For instance, "By implementing a new project management tool, I increased team productivity by 20%." These specific examples show how your work directly impacts the organization's goals.

- **Demonstrating Personal Worth**: Practice saying your value statements with confidence. For example, "My ability to lead cross-functional teams has consistently resulted in projects being completed ahead of schedule and under budget." Clear, powerful statements like this position you as a valuable asset to any organization.

Creating a Brag Book

A **brag book** is a powerful tool that helps you document and present your achievements effectively during key moments, like salary negotiations (Guerin, 2014). By showcasing your accomplishments, you provide concrete evidence to support your requests. For instance, you could say, *"As highlighted in my performance reviews, I led a project that improved efficiency by 15%. Given this and market research, I believe a salary adjustment is justified."*

Here's how to create and use a brag book:

1. What is a Brag Book?

A brag book is a curated collection of documents that highlights your professional accomplishments, skills, and experiences. It's a tangible reflection of your value and can be used in situations such as job interviews, performance reviews, and salary negotiations to provide proof of your contributions.

2. Contents of a Brag Book:

- **Resume and Cover Letter**: Include your most updated resume and a thoughtfully written cover letter.

- **Certificates and Awards**: Add any certifications, training completions, or awards that demonstrate your growth and achievements.

- **Performance Reviews**: Include positive feedback or evaluations from supervisors and colleagues to showcase your performance.

- **Project Summaries**: Document key projects you've led or contributed to, focusing on your role and the successful outcomes.

- **Testimonials and References**: Gather testimonials or reference letters from supervisors, clients, or coworkers that highlight your strengths and contributions.

3. Using a Brag Book:

- **During Interviews**: Use your brag book to provide real examples of your accomplishments and skills.

- **Performance Reviews**: Refer to it during performance reviews to clearly demonstrate your impact and support your case for promotions or raises.

- **Salary Negotiations**: Present your brag book during salary discussions to substantiate your request and show the value you bring to the organization.

Negotiation Strategies: Presenting Your Case Assertively and Professionally

When negotiating, presenting your case with clarity and professionalism is key (Shell, 2006). Here's how to structure your negotiation approach for the best results:

1. Prepare Your Talking Points

Preparation is the foundation of a successful negotiation. You need to have clear, concise talking points that summarize your research and personal achievements:

- **Research and Evidence**: Gather information about industry salary standards and your contributions. For example, *"Based on industry research, the average salary for this role is $X. Additionally, my contributions, such as [specific achievements], have significantly impacted team success, justifying my salary request."*

- **Logical Structure**: Organize your points. Start with research, follow with your key accomplishments, and finish with your specific salary request. This ensures a clear, persuasive presentation.

2. Practice Active Listening

- **Engaged Listening**: Active listening shows you're taking your employer's concerns into account. For instance, if budget constraints are a concern, respond with, "I understand budget is a concern. How might we address this while considering my request?" This fosters a collaborative discussion.

3. Use a Collaborative Approach

- **Frame as a Partnership**: Frame the negotiation as a partnership, focusing on mutual benefits. For example, "By aligning my compensation with my contributions, we can ensure continued success together. How can we find a solution that works for both of us?"

4. Maintain Professionalism

- **Stay Composed**: Remain calm and respectful, even if faced with challenges (Fisher & Ury, 1981). For example, "I appreciate your feedback and understand the constraints. Let's explore how we can address both our needs effectively." Maintaining a professional tone keeps the discussion productive.

5. Highlight Future Contributions

Negotiating your salary isn't just about past achievements; it's also about the value you'll bring in the future.

- **Future-Oriented Thinking**: Clearly outline how your salary request aligns with your anticipated contributions. For example, "With the proposed salary adjustment, I am confident I can drive growth in our department through [specific projects or goals], which will significantly contribute to our overall success." This positions you as a forward-thinking asset to the organization.

- **Discuss Future Initiatives**: As the conversation progresses, introduce projects you're excited to lead. For instance, "Looking ahead, I'm eager to take on [X initiative], which I believe will have a significant impact on our team's success. This is an opportunity to align my compensation with the value I will bring moving forward."

As you assert your worth and engage in salary negotiations, it's essential to maintain a foundation of mutual respect and professionalism. However, not all negotiations occur on equal terms. In some instances, inappropriate requests or implications may surface, making it critical to recognize when professional boundaries are being crossed. This brings us to the next important discussion: understanding and addressing quid pro quo situations, where professional advancement may be unfairly tied to personal favors.

Addressing Quid Pro Quo Situations

Defining Quid Pro Quo

Quid pro quo, meaning "something for something" in Latin, often refers to situations in the workplace where job benefits—such as salary increases or promotions—are contingent upon providing personal favors, typically of a sexual nature (Gutman, 2017). This form of harassment is illegal, unethical, and undermines the integrity of professional relationships.

Handling Implications for Personal Favors

- **Recognizing the Signs**: Be vigilant about situations where salary increases or promotions are implied to be tied to personal favors, whether subtle or overt. Early recognition is crucial.

- **Using Professional Language**: Assert your boundaries while maintaining professionalism. For example, "I believe my performance should be evaluated based on my work, not personal matters."

- **Staying Firm**: If faced with inappropriate requests, remain clear and assertive. For instance, "I am committed to my role and prefer to keep our interactions strictly professional."

Understanding and Setting Boundaries

- **Recognize Quid Pro Quo**: Awareness is key to maintaining your integrity in these situations.

- **Firmly Decline Inappropriate Requests**: Clearly decline inappropriate favors. For example, "I am not comfortable with this request. Let's keep our relationship focused on professional matters."

- **Establish Clear Boundaries**: Communicate clear boundaries while preserving professionalism. For instance, "I value our working relationship and believe it's important to maintain clear boundaries for mutual respect."

The **2 AM Code** teaches you to stand firm in your worth. By advocating for yourself with confidence and clarity, you ensure that your value is recognized without compromising your integrity.

Documenting Conversations

Maintaining a detailed record of all interactions during salary negotiations, as well as any inappropriate comments or requests, is critical for protecting yourself legally and professionally (Edelman et al., 1993).

1. **Keep Records**

   - Document all relevant conversations, including salary discussions and any inappropriate comments. Save emails, meeting notes, and any other communications that pertain to your case.

2. **Detail the Context**

   ◻ Record key details such as who was present, what was discussed, and the responses given. This documentation can serve as crucial evidence if future issues arise.

Seeking Support and Resources

1. **HR Support**

   ◻ If faced with quid pro quo situations, report them to your HR department. HR can provide guidance and take appropriate action to address the issue.

2. **Career Coaching**

   ◻ Seek external career coaching for tailored advice and strategies on handling difficult situations. Career coaches can offer independent perspectives and support.

3. **Online Resources**

   ◻ Use platforms like the Equal Employment Opportunity Commission (EEOC) to understand your rights and access resources that address workplace harassment.

Championing Your Worth

In this chapter, we emphasized the importance of recognizing and advocating for your worth, both personally and professionally. By understanding your value, setting clear expectations, and communicating your contributions, you can build a fulfilling career on your own terms.

The 2 AM Code empowers you to stand firm in your worth, ensuring that you advocate for yourself confidently and assertively. Every negotiation becomes an opportunity to assert your value with The Code guiding you to remain grounded in self-respect and integrity.

As you reflect on how effectively you are advocating for your worth, the following assessment will help you evaluate your current practices and identify areas for improvement. This is your opportunity to assert your value and ensure that your contributions are recognized and respected.

ASSESSMENT: SALARY NEGOTIATION CONFIDENCE SCALE

Instructions: Rate each statement on a scale from 1 (Strongly disagree) to 5 (Strongly agree).

1. I feel confident discussing my salary with my employer.
2. I can clearly articulate my value and contributions.
3. I am comfortable negotiating for a higher salary.
4. I know how to research and present market salary data.
5. I can handle objections and counteroffers effectively.
6. I prepare thoroughly for salary negotiations.
7. I can remain calm and composed during negotiations.
8. I understand the importance of timing in salary discussions.
9. I can negotiate other benefits if salary increases are not possible.
10. I feel empowered to advocate for my financial worth.

Advocating for Yourself: Salary Negotiation

Scoring Interpretation

- 10-20: Low Confidence in Salary Negotiation

Description: Individuals in this range may feel uncomfortable discussing their salary and lack confidence in negotiating for higher pay. They might struggle to articulate their value and handle objections effectively.

Action Steps:

1. Research Salary Benchmarks: Learn about salary benchmarks in your industry to understand your market value.

2. Practice Negotiation Scenarios: Role-play salary negotiations with a friend or mentor to build confidence.

3. Prepare Thoroughly: Make a list of your achievements and contributions to present during negotiations.

- 21-35: Moderate Confidence in Salary Negotiation

Description: Individuals in this range have moderate confidence in salary negotiation. They can discuss their salary and negotiate for higher pay in most situations but may still experience occasional discomfort.

Action Steps:

1. Reflect on Past Negotiations: Think about past salary negotiations and what you can learn from them.

2. Role-Play Scenarios: Continue practicing negotiation scenarios to build confidence.

3. Seek Feedback: Ask for feedback from trusted colleagues or mentors on your negotiation approach.

- 36-50: High Confidence in Salary Negotiation

Description: Individuals in this range are highly confident in salary negotiation. They can discuss their salary, articulate their value, and handle objections effectively. They feel empowered to advocate for their financial worth.

Action Steps:

1. Continue Advocating Confidently: Maintain your confidence in salary negotiations.

2. Share Strategies: Help others develop their salary negotiation skills by sharing your strategies.

3. Reflect on Successes: Regularly reflect on your negotiation experiences and celebrate your successes.

Congratulations! You've unlocked strategies for confidently negotiating your salary, helping you take ownership of your financial future and professional worth. With these negotiation tactics in hand, you're ready to approach compensation conversations with clarity and strength.

Now, it's time to build on this by cultivating a **robust professional support network**. In **Chapter 10**, we'll explore how you can expand your circle, foster valuable connections, and leverage relationships to advance your career.

10

CULTIVATING CONNECTIONS: BUILDING A ROBUST PROFESSIONAL SUPPORT NETWORK

In the journey of professional growth, building connections isn't just about increasing your contacts—it's about fostering relationships that propel your career forward. History is filled with examples of individuals who leveraged their networks to achieve remarkable success. Mark Zuckerberg's rise with Facebook was significantly bolstered by the mentorship of Steve Jobs, the strategic guidance of early investors like Peter Thiel, and the collaborative environment of Silicon Valley (Kirkpatrick, 2010). These connections provided invaluable insights, resources, and support, helping him navigate the challenges of scaling a tech startup.

A strong professional network offers numerous benefits—career advancement, access to valuable resources, mentorship, and referrals that can open new doors (Ibarra & Hunter, 2007). However, cultivating such a network requires intentional effort and a strategic approach. By identifying your networking goals, leveraging online platforms, attending industry events, and prioritizing quality relationships over sheer numbers, you can build a support system that enhances your professional growth and satisfaction.

Remember, networking is a two-way street. Offering support, maintaining regular communication, and celebrating the successes of others are essential to fostering meaningful connections. By embracing the responsibility of cultivating a supportive network, you enrich your professional life and establish relationships that stand the test of time.

The Importance of Community

In the modern workplace, having a supportive community is essential for both personal and professional growth. Allies within your organization create an environment where individuals feel valued and empowered. These networks may come from colleagues, professional associations, or acquaintances. By promoting mutual support, women can share experiences, amplify each other's voices, and foster a sense of belonging that helps everyone thrive (Ely, Ibarra, & Kolb, 2011).

Building a professional network requires intention and resilience. The **2 AM Code** serves as a reminder that standing up for yourself also means building a circle that respects your boundaries, honors your voice, and celebrates your victories. Let's explore how to strategically cultivate a professional support system that not only uplifts you but also strengthens others in your circle.

As you build your professional network, remember that every connection you make is not just a contact but an ally in your journey. The power of community lies in its ability to support, uplift, and collaborate. Your network is the extension of the safe spaces you create—a circle where your boundaries are respected, your voice is valued, and your goals are shared. Now, let's dive into the steps to strategically cultivate this powerful support system.

The Value of a Professional Support Network

Career Advancement

- **Historical Examples**: Throughout history, influential figures like Benjamin Franklin and Eleanor Roosevelt used their networks to achieve great success (Isaacson, 2033). Franklin's Junto Club—a group of like-minded individuals—was pivotal in his personal and professional growth.

- **Modern Application**: Today, a strong network provides access to mentorship, industry insights, and resources that can open doors to career advancement and professional growth.

Steps to Building a Professional Network

Identify Your Goals

Before you step into the world of networking, take a moment to center yourself in your purpose. What is your vision? What heights are you aiming to reach? Whether you're looking for mentorship, industry expertise, or fresh career opportunities, defining your goals is the key to unlocking intentional and powerful connections (Ibarra & Hunter, 2007). Your aspirations are your compass, guiding you toward relationships that not only support your journey but elevate it.

Remember, your professional path is yours alone—unique and filled with potential. When you articulate your goals, you're not just setting direction; you're claiming your right to pursue relationships that align with your true worth. *The 2 AM Code* teaches you that clarity in purpose empowers you to engage with intention, ensuring every connection is a step toward the greatness you're building.

Leverage Online Platforms

Platforms like LinkedIn and industry forums offer opportunities to connect, collaborate, and learn from professionals worldwide (Briggs, 2016). Each connection is more than just an addition to your contact list—it's a strategic move toward collaboration, learning, and mutual growth. By stepping into these spaces with confidence, you don't just expand your network; you cultivate a community of driven, like-minded professionals who challenge you, uplift you, and open doors you hadn't imagined.

The 2 AM Code reminds you that every tool at your disposal is an opportunity. The power to connect, to grow, and to elevate lies in your hands. Use these platforms to create relationships that reflect your values and ambitions, making each connection a reflection of the empowered future you're crafting.

While online platforms provide global access to mentors, collaborators, and industry leaders, sometimes there's no substitute for in-person connections. Industry events offer you the chance to bring those digital relationships to life, creating opportunities to strengthen your presence in the room and align with thought leaders face-to-face.

Attend Industry Events

Think of industry events—conferences, seminars, and workshops— as modern salons of exchange and influence, places where thought leaders gather to spark innovation and growth (Uzzi & Dunlap, 2005). These spaces are rich with opportunity, filled with individuals who are shaping your field. By attending these events, you step into the very heart of your industry, positioning yourself among the key players, and forging relationships that have the potential to transform your career.

The 2 AM Code inspires you to surround yourself with empowered networks, where collaboration and mutual respect thrive. Together, we rise by lifting each other, creating spaces where every voice is heard, valued, and celebrated. These events are your chance to immerse yourself in communities that share your vision for success, offering you both the platform and the support to take your professional journey to the next level.

Building Meaningful Relationships

Quality Over Quantity

Networking isn't about how many people you know, but how deeply you know them (Cross & Thomas, 2008). Focus on building meaningful, trusted relationships by taking the time to understand others' goals, interests, and challenges. This depth fosters mutual respect, making your network a valuable resource for both parties.

Offer Support

Networking is a reciprocal process. Be proactive in offering help, resources, and advice to others (Baker, 2000). When you support others, they're more likely to support you in return. For example, if a colleague is seeking a job, offer to review their resume or introduce them to someone in your network.

Follow Up

Consistency is key. After meeting someone new, follow up with a personalized message to reinforce the connection (Zetlin, 2018). For example, "It was great to meet you at the conference. I enjoyed our conversation about [specific topic]. Let's stay in touch and explore potential collaboration." Regular follow-ups demonstrate your commitment to maintaining the relationship.

Maintaining Your Network

Regular Check-Ins

Just as iconic figures like Thomas Jefferson and John Adams strengthened their bonds through consistent correspondence, nurturing your network requires intentional, ongoing communication (Ellis, 1996). Make it a priority to schedule regular check-ins—monthly or quarterly—to stay connected with those in your circle. These conversations go beyond mere updates; they reaffirm the foundation of trust, support, and mutual growth. Each check-in is a reminder that you're actively cultivating a community where everyone's journey is respected, and every step forward is celebrated together. You are the architect of these relationships, and by maintaining them, you ensure that your network remains a source of empowerment and opportunity.

Share Valuable Content

Your network thrives not only through personal connection but through the value you bring to it (Ibarra, 2015). Sharing relevant industry insights, articles, or breakthroughs positions you as a vital resource within your circle. When you come across information that speaks to a contact's interests or goals, don't hesitate to send it along with a thoughtful note. This isn't just about staying visible—it's about uplifting others with knowledge that can further their journey. Every time you share value, you reinforce your role as a leader who not only seeks growth for herself but for everyone in her community. The 2 AM Code teaches you that generosity in knowledge is an act of empowerment—what you give to others, you multiply in return.

Celebrate Successes

In a world that often overlooks personal victories, The 2 AM Code encourages you to actively celebrate the achievements of those around you. When someone in your network reaches a milestone— whether it's a promotion, a successful project, or a personal break-through—recognize it. Send a congratulatory message, share their success on social media, or reach out with heartfelt words of encouragement. Celebrating others is a powerful way to strengthen your bond and foster an environment of support and respect (Hallowell, 2011). By honoring their wins, you're affirming that success is not a zero-sum game—when one of us rises, we all rise. In every celebration, you weave a tighter, more resilient network that thrives on shared victories.

Leveraging Your Network for Career Growth

Seek Mentorship

Just as Alexander the Great sought wisdom from Aristotle, find mentors who can guide your career development (Kram, 1985). Approach potential mentors with a clear idea of what you hope to gain and what you can offer in return.

Collaborate on Projects

Look for opportunities to collaborate with your network on projects. Whether co-authoring an article or launching a joint initiative, collaboration strengthens your relationships and showcases your abilities (Kelley & Caplan, 1993).

Ask for Referrals

Don't hesitate to ask for job referrals or introductions to key industry players (Granovetter, 1973). Be specific about what you're seeking and why, making it easier for your contacts to help.

Overcoming Networking Challenges

Step Out of Your Comfort Zone

Growth happens outside your comfort zone. Attend new events and connect with individuals beyond your immediate circle (Brown, 2013). This broadens your horizons and presents new opportunities.

Be Authentic

Authenticity fosters trust. Be genuine in your interactions, share your true self, and show sincere interest in others (Goffee & Jones, 2006). People are drawn to authenticity, and it strengthens your professional relationships.

Manage Networking Fatigue

Building and maintaining a strong professional network is a powerful journey, one that thrives in a safe, inclusive environment (Pfeffer, 2010). To truly excel, it's essential to prioritize balance, ensuring both you and your connections feel supported and respected. Safe spaces go beyond the physical—they are emotional and mental environments that empower you to engage authentically and confidently, free from the pressure of constant availability. When you honor these spaces, you allow yourself to show up fully, ensuring that your interactions remain genuine and meaningful.

Effective networking begins with setting boundaries that protect your energy and well-being. *The 2 AM Code* reminds you that maintaining your personal safe space is crucial for sustaining your strength and value within your network. Success isn't measured by attending every event or constantly being "on"—it's about being intentional, present, and aligned with your true self. By limiting your commitments and allowing time to recharge, you foster mutual respect and growth in your connections.

When you honor your needs and prioritize self-care, you create the foundation for deeper, more meaningful relationships—connections built on trust, respect, and mutual empowerment. You don't need constant connectivity to build a powerful network. Your value shines brightest in authentic, mindful engagements that respect your boundaries. The safe spaces you create aren't just supportive—they are key to building a network that uplifts, sustains, and propels you toward success.

Maintaining a strong network isn't just about staying in touch—it's about nurturing an environment of respect, trust, and safety. These connections will flourish when rooted in the safe spaces you create, both in your professional and personal life. Let's explore how cultivating these spaces can deepen and strengthen your professional relationships.

Creating Safe Spaces

Creating safe spaces, both in the workplace and in personal life, is crucial for fostering trust, open communication, and overall well-being. A safe space is an environment where individuals feel empowered to express themselves freely, without fear of judgment or retaliation. It nurtures healthy relationships and builds a culture of inclusivity and respect (Edmondson, 2019).

Safe Spaces in the Workplace

A psychologically safe workplace empowers employees to share ideas freely, fostering creativity and honest dialogue (Edmondson, 1999). Here are key strategies to build such a space:

- **Build Trust**: Trust is the foundation of any safe space. Leaders should model open and honest communication, keep their commitments, and foster an atmosphere where confidentiality is respected.

- **Foster Respect**: Cultivate a culture that values diverse perspectives and treats everyone with dignity. Encourage active listening, empathy, and understanding, even when opinions differ. A respectful environment empowers everyone to contribute without hesitation.

- **Encourage Vulnerability**: Leaders can set the tone by being open and vulnerable themselves. Creating opportunities for team members to share their experiences and challenges allows for deeper connections and a sense of belonging.
- **Co-Create Rules of Engagement**: Collaborate with employees to establish guidelines for respectful interactions. When everyone participates in setting these ground rules, they feel more invested in maintaining a supportive and safe environment.

Safe Spaces in Personal Life

Just as in the workplace, creating safe spaces in your personal life is essential for nurturing healthy, fulfilling relationships (Brene, 2015). Here's how you can do it:

- **Communicate Openly**: Foster a culture of open and honest communication with family and friends. Encourage sharing of thoughts and feelings without fear of judgment, and model that openness in your own interactions.
- **Set Boundaries**: Clearly establish boundaries that protect your well-being and personal space. Communicate them with respect and ensure they are honored by others.
- **Practice Empathy**: Listen actively and show empathy towards others, even when you don't fully agree. Validating their feelings helps build deeper connections and trust.
- **Create Rituals of Connection**: Develop habits that reinforce connection and safety, such as regular family dinners, date nights, or check-ins with friends. These rituals offer a structured way to maintain communication and support.

The Impact of Safe Spaces

The benefits of creating safe spaces are profound, both professionally and personally:

- **In the Workplace**: A psychologically safe environment fosters greater collaboration, innovation, and overall team success. When people feel safe, they contribute more freely, share their best ideas, and engage in meaningful discussions.

- **In Personal Life**: Safe spaces in your personal relationships lead to deeper connections, trust, and emotional well-being. They allow people to be their true selves, resulting in more authentic and fulfilling relationships.

In male-dominated industries, safe spaces can be hard to find, but one of the most powerful ways to create them is through mentorship. By seeking guidance from experienced mentors who understand the challenges of navigating these spaces, you can develop the resilience and support needed to not only survive but thrive. Let's explore how mentorship can serve as a cornerstone of these safe, empowering environments.

Creating a Safe Space in a Male-Dominated Industry

In male-dominated industries, fostering a safe and inclusive space is essential for empowering women and creating a workplace where everyone feels valued and respected. This can be achieved through open communication, promoting diversity, encouraging collaboration, active intervention, and leading by example. By adopting these strategies, organizations can build environments where every voice is heard, and all employees can thrive.

Here are key approaches to establishing such spaces, along with insights from women who have successfully created supportive networks in their fields.

1. Establish Clear Communication Channels

Creating a safe space starts with establishing open and honest lines of communication. It's important to provide opportunities for individuals to share their thoughts, concerns, and ideas without fear of judgment or reprisal.

- **Insight**: "In my team, we hold regular check-in meetings where everyone can share their thoughts on projects and workplace dynamics. This fosters an environment where feedback is welcomed, and we can discuss issues openly," shares Sara Thompson, a project manager in a tech firm.

- **Quote**: "A safe space is one where communication flows freely, and everyone feels empowered to share their perspectives." — Dr. Elaine Carter, Leadership Coach.

2. Promote Diversity and Inclusion Initiatives

A diverse and inclusive workplace is essential for safety. Organizations should actively champion initiatives that support women and underrepresented groups.

- **Actions to Take:**
  - Establish mentorship programs pairing women with experienced leaders in the industry.
  - Create employee resource groups (ERGs) that offer support and networking opportunities for underrepresented employees.

- **Insight**: "Having a women's network within our company has been instrumental. It provides a platform for sharing experiences and strategies for overcoming challenges," states Maria Gomez, an engineer in the construction industry.

- **Quote**: "Diversity isn't just about numbers; it's about creating an environment where everyone can thrive." — Chandra Lee, Diversity and Inclusion Consultant.

3. Foster Collaborative Relationships

Building trust and collaboration among team members is a powerful way to create a sense of safety in the workplace. When team members support one another, it strengthens the overall work culture.

- **Team-building Activities**:
  - Organize exercises that encourage bonding and understanding among colleagues.
  - Engage in collaborative projects where diverse perspectives are required to achieve success.

- **Insight**: "When we shifted our focus to collaboration instead of competition, the atmosphere transformed. We became a team that supports one another, and it made a huge difference," notes Jessica Tran, a software developer.

- **Quote**: "Collaboration breeds trust, and trust is the foundation of a safe space." — Hannah Kim, Human Resources Manager.

4. Encourage Active Bystander Intervention

Empowering employees to step in when they witness inappropriate behavior is essential for maintaining a safe and accountable workplace. Training staff to recognize and address harassment or exclusionary actions ensures that everyone plays a role in upholding respect.

- **Training Programs**:

  - Implement sessions on bystander intervention strategies, teaching employees how to speak up when they witness disrespectful behavior.

- **Insight**: "We had a workshop on bystander intervention that equipped us with the tools to address issues in the moment. It made a significant impact on how we interact," says Linda Patel, a financial analyst.

- **Quote**: "It's not enough to be non-discriminatory; we must be actively anti-discriminatory." — Renee Oliver, Advocate for Workplace Equity.

5. Lead by Example

Leadership is critical to creating and sustaining safe spaces. Leaders must model inclusive behavior and champion initiatives that promote safety and respect for all employees.

- **Leadership Actions**:

  - Hold leaders accountable for fostering an inclusive and respectful culture.
  - Encourage leaders to actively engage with all team members, ensuring that everyone's voice is heard and valued.

- **Insight**: "Our leadership team has made a conscious effort to include diverse voices in discussions. It sends a strong message that everyone's input matters," remarks Tina Nguyen, a marketing director.

- **Quote**: "True leadership is about creating a culture where everyone feels safe to speak up." — James Wright, Executive Coach.

Utilizing Mentorship

Mentorship is one of the most powerful tools for professional and personal growth. By seeking guidance from mentors, you can gain valuable insights, develop new skills, and strengthen your support network. Let's explore how to make the most of mentorship to foster a safe, empowering environment that encourages growth and connection (Kram, 1985).

The Power of Mentorship

Mentorship offers the chance to learn from others' wisdom, guiding you through the complexities of career and personal growth. Studies show that having a mentor significantly increases the likelihood of achieving professional goals and experiencing higher job satisfaction. It's not just about receiving advice—mentorship is about building a relationship that promotes mutual growth and respect.

Seeking Guidance from Mentors

Identify Potential Mentors

- **Look Within Your Network**: Start by identifying potential mentors in your existing circles—whether it's colleagues, supervisors, or industry leaders who have the experience and insight you admire.

- **Expand Your Search**: If suitable mentors aren't within your immediate network, expand your search to professional organizations, industry events, or online platforms like LinkedIn. Sometimes the perfect mentor is one step beyond your current connections.

Approach with Intent

- **Clarify Your Goals**: When approaching a mentor, be clear about what you hope to achieve. Whether it's gaining industry insight, career advancement, or personal development, a clear vision sets the stage for a productive and mutually beneficial mentorship.

- **Show Respect and Appreciation**: Respect your mentor's expertise and express gratitude for their time. Acknowledging their guidance not only fosters a positive dynamic but also shows that you value the relationship.

Leverage Community and Networks

Join Professional Groups

- **Engage in Professional Communities**: Becoming active in groups that align with your career interests can provide access to mentorship programs, networking events, and resources that support your development. Many professional communities have formal mentorship programs where experienced members guide emerging professionals.

Collaborate and Share

- **Contribute Your Knowledge**: Mentorship isn't just about receiving wisdom—it's also about sharing your own knowledge and experiences. Engage actively in discussions, offer support, and be open to collaboration. This approach not only strengthens your network but also positions you as a valuable member of the community.

Mentorship as a Two-Way Street

Offer Support

- **Reciprocal Value**: While mentors provide guidance, it's important to offer something in return (Ragins & Kram, 2007). Whether it's sharing fresh perspectives, providing feedback, or assisting with projects, a reciprocal relationship enriches the mentorship for both parties. Mentorship works best when there's mutual benefit and respect.

Celebrate Success Together

- **Acknowledge Milestones**: Celebrate the milestones and successes that come out of your mentorship. Recognizing these achievements strengthens the bond and motivates ongoing growth. Whether it's a promotion, a project completion, or personal breakthrough, celebrating together fosters a positive, lasting relationship.

In this chapter, we've explored the art of cultivating connections and building a strong professional support network. Meaningful relationships can open doors, provide essential support, and significantly impact your career trajectory. From effective networking strategies to the importance of maintaining authentic relationships, these connections serve as a foundation for both professional and personal growth.

Now, it's time to reflect on how well you're nurturing your network. The following assessment will guide you in evaluating your current networking practices and help you identify areas where you can deepen your connections. As you complete the assessment, think about how your network has shaped your career—and how you can continue to strengthen this vital aspect of your journey.

BUILDING A SUPPORT NETWORK ASSESSMENT: SUPPORT NETWORK STRENGTH SCALE

Instructions: Rate each statement on a scale from 1 (Strongly disagree) to 5 (Strongly agree).

1. I have a strong professional support network.
2. I can rely on my network for advice and guidance.
3. I actively seek to expand my professional connections.
4. I offer support and mentorship to others in my network.
5. I feel confident in leveraging my network for career growth.
6. I regularly attend networking events.
7. I maintain regular contact with my professional connections.
8. I can ask for help when needed.
9. I provide value to my network through knowledge and resources.
10. I feel a sense of community within my professional network.

Chapter 10: Building a Support Network

Scoring Interpretation

- 10-20: Weak Support Network

   Description: Individuals in this range may have a limited professional support network. They might struggle to rely on others for advice and guidance and may not actively seek to expand their connections.

Action Steps:

   1. Attend Networking Events: Participate in industry conferences, seminars, and networking events to meet new people.

2. Join Professional Organizations: Become a member of professional organizations related to your field.

3. Reach Out to Colleagues: Initiate conversations with colleagues and industry professionals to build relationships.

- 21-35: Moderate Support Network

Description: Individuals in this range have a moderate support network. They can rely on their network for advice and guidance in most situations but may not fully leverage their connections for career growth.

Action Steps:

1. Strengthen Existing Connections: Keep in regular contact with your professional connections through emails, calls, or meetings.

2. Offer Support: Provide help and mentorship to others in your network to strengthen relationships.

3. Expand Your Network: Continue to seek opportunities to meet new people and expand your professional network.

- 36-50: Strong Support Network

Description: Individuals in this range have a strong professional support network. They can rely on their network for advice, guidance, and career growth opportunities. They actively seek to expand and nurture their connections.

Action Steps:

1. Continue Nurturing Your Network: Maintain and strengthen your professional relationships.

2. Mentor Others: Share your knowledge and experience by mentoring others in your network.

3. Facilitate Connections: Help connect people within your network to foster a sense of community and collaboration.

You've now learned the art of building and maintaining a strong professional network. These connections are vital to your career growth and will provide you with support, advice, and new opportunities. With your network-building skills sharpened, you're well-positioned to foster meaningful relationships that will enrich your career journey.

Next, we'll dive into how you can use **digital empowerment** to further your professional success. In **Chapter 11**, we'll explore how to leverage technology to enhance your visibility, productivity, and influence in today's fast-paced, tech-driven world.

CHAPTER

11

DIGITAL EMPOWERMENT: LEVERAGING TECHNOLOGY FOR PROFESSIONAL ADVANCEMENT

In today's fast-paced digital world, artificial intelligence (AI) is driving innovation and creating unprecedented opportunities for career growth and development. For women, AI is more than just a tool—it's a powerful ally in breaking down barriers and leveling the playing field in the workplace. By leveraging AI, women can enhance their productivity, make informed decisions, and access career paths that were once out of reach.

This chapter explores how AI empowers women to navigate their careers with confidence and efficiency, turning challenges into opportunities and fostering a more inclusive, equitable professional environment. With AI, women can unlock new possibilities, positioning themselves for success in a rapidly evolving landscape.

AI Conversations: Crafting a Blueprint for Women's Empowerment

Empowering Conversations: How AI Helped Me Write a Book to Empower Women

Amid a hectic schedule, I felt a strong desire to write a book that would empower women to navigate the complexities of the workplace. Though the vision was clear, the journey seemed daunting—until I turned to AI. This technology became an invaluable partner in transforming my ideas into reality.

AI allowed me to have insightful conversations on topics I didn't have time to research in depth, from self-efficacy and assertiveness to setting boundaries and handling professional challenges. These interactions didn't just provide knowledge; they were transformative, helping me refine my thoughts and organize key concepts (Batra et al., 2020). Whenever I felt overwhelmed, AI was there to distill the vast information, highlight the essentials, and suggest innovative ways to present them. It became my 24/7 personal assistant, always ready to help.

AI's role went beyond organizing information; it helped me communicate more effectively. Whether it was finding the right words to convey complex ideas or crafting responses to difficult situations, AI provided empathetic, actionable guidance. This was especially valuable when dealing with unwanted advances in the workplace, where AI offered strategies for assertive, professional responses that boosted my confidence in handling such issues.

As the book evolved, AI became more than a tool—it became a collaborator, challenging my perspectives and helping me create content that truly resonated. The end result was a book that empowers women to assert their worth and navigate the workplace with confidence and grace. This journey of growth and empowerment wouldn't have been possible without the unique capabilities of AI.

Through AI, women can not only enhance their abilities but also take control of their careers. It provides the tools for personal and professional success while fostering an inclusive, supportive environment where women can thrive. By opening doors to knowledge and solutions, AI becomes an essential ally in advancing women's empowerment.

Understanding Artificial Intelligence

Artificial Intelligence (AI) refers to the simulation of human intelligence in machines that are programmed to think and learn like humans. These intelligent systems can perform tasks that typically require human intelligence, such as recognizing speech, making decisions, solving problems, and even understanding natural language (Russell & Norvig, 2020).

AI is powered by algorithms and vast amounts of data, enabling machines to learn from experience, adapt to new inputs, and perform human-like tasks with increasing accuracy. There are several types of AI, including:

1. Narrow AI: Designed to perform a specific task, such as virtual assistants like Siri or Alexa.

2. General AI: A more advanced form of AI that can perform any intellectual task that a human can do. This type of AI is still largely theoretical.

3. Machine Learning: A subset of AI that involves training algorithms to learn from and make predictions based on data.

4. Deep Learning: A more complex form of machine learning that uses neural networks with many layers to analyze various factors of data.

Understanding these AI types equips women to see how these technologies are transforming industries and careers. With this knowledge, they can apply AI strategically—whether it's leveraging machine learning to extract insights from data or using virtual assistants like Siri and Alexa to streamline tasks and boost productivity (Kumar et al., 2019).

For women in data-driven roles, understanding how machine learning algorithms predict outcomes helps turn data into actionable insights, enhancing decision-making and planning. In creative or content-focused careers, AI automates routine tasks like content scheduling or customer inquiries, freeing up time for innovation and leadership.

The key is not just to learn about AI but to harness it with intention. The 2 AM Code is about owning your power in every aspect of your career, and AI is a vital tool that helps women do just that—whether it's boosting productivity, unlocking new opportunities, or managing their careers more effectively. AI enables women to redefine how they work, collaborate, and lead, giving them the confidence to thrive on their own terms.

AI Empowerment: Navigating Career Paths with Confidence and Support

Artificial Intelligence (AI) is transforming the workplace, offering powerful tools that not only boost productivity but create environments where women can truly thrive. By embracing AI, women can step into their careers with confidence, clarity, and a sense of purpose (West, 2018). Here's how AI empowers women to take charge of their professional journeys:

1. **Confident Decision-Making**: AI delivers data-driven insights that empower women to make bold, informed choices—whether it's selecting a new career path, negotiating a well-deserved raise, or identifying the next growth opportunity. With AI, you can trust that your decisions are grounded in facts, giving you the edge to push forward.

2. **Maximizing Productivity Without Burnout**: By automating routine tasks, AI frees up your time and energy, allowing you to focus on the strategic, creative work that moves your career forward. You're not just working harder—you're working smarter, with AI ensuring that you stay productive without burning out.

3. **Personalized Learning and Growth**: AI tailors learning experiences to your unique needs, enabling you to acquire new skills at your own pace. This personalized approach ensures that you're always growing, evolving, and ready for the next challenge in your career.

4. **Achieving Work-Life Harmony**: AI-driven tools help you organize and optimize your time, making it easier to balance professional responsibilities with your personal life. With AI's support, you can excel at work while maintaining the harmony that keeps you grounded and fulfilled.

5. **Creating Inclusive Spaces**: AI plays a pivotal role in reducing workplace biases, fostering an environment where your voice is heard, and your contributions are respected(Sunstein, 2019). It's about leveling the playing field and creating a space where you are valued for your true worth.

6. **Expanding Your Networks and Mentorship Opportunities**: AI connects you to the mentors and professional networks that fuel your career growth. With the right support system in place, you're empowered to build meaningful relationships that elevate both your career and your confidence.

7. **Equitable Hiring and Promotions**: AI helps remove the subjectivity from hiring and promotion processes, focusing on your skills, qualifications, and achievements. This paves the way for more equitable opportunities and ensures you're judged on your merits.

8. **Safety and Support in the Workplace**: AI-powered tools can monitor workplace interactions and detect early signs of harassment or inappropriate behavior, helping create a safer, more supportive environment. With AI on your side, you can work confidently knowing your well-being is protected.

9. **Empowerment Through Actionable Insights**: With AI's ability to analyze industry trends, salary benchmarks, and career data, you have the information you need to negotiate better terms and make empowered career decisions. Knowledge is power, and AI equips you with the insights to take control.

10. **Seamless Collaboration and Leadership**: AI enhances communication and collaboration across teams, breaking down geographic and organizational barriers. With AI, you can lead global projects, contribute effectively, and build strong professional relationships, no matter where your team is located.

AI isn't just a tool for boosting efficiency—it's a game-changer that redefines professional empowerment. When you harness the full potential of AI, you're not just opening doors—you're taking control of your career, creating opportunities, and confidently shaping your future. *The 2 AM Code* is about standing in your power, and with AI, you have the tools to rise to new heights.

Mastering Digital Tools for Career Success

Mastering digital tools isn't just about building skills; it's about stepping into your power, owning your expertise, and leading with confidence (Codagnone et al., 2018). These tools give you the ability to not only transform your career but also position yourself as a leader who shapes the future. By harnessing digital literacy, you're amplifying your impact, driving innovation, and fully embracing your potential. Let's explore how digital literacy and tech skills empower women to excel and thrive.

1. Digital Skills and Literacy for AI

The Importance of Digital Literacy

In today's rapidly evolving job market, being tech-savvy is no longer optional—it's essential. Digital literacy is the key to staying competitive and relevant in an increasingly tech-driven world. Here's how mastering these tools empowers you to lead and succeed:

- **Competitive Edge**: Mastering digital tools doesn't just make you a skilled professional; it makes you a leader in your field. As businesses rely more on digital platforms, the ability to navigate these tools makes you a sought-after candidate who can drive success in any industry.

- **Career Opportunities**: From technology to marketing and data analysis, digital skills open doors to roles that didn't exist before. By embracing these skills, you're not just growing in your career—you're becoming a leader in emerging fields.

- **Adaptability**: In a landscape that's constantly changing, adaptability is key. Being fluent in digital tools ensures that you stay ahead of the curve, maintaining your relevance and demonstrating the agility that every leader needs.

- **Efficiency and Productivity**: Digital tools streamline workflows, automate tasks, and give you more time to focus on strategic initiatives. By mastering these tools, you're boosting your productivity and showing leadership through efficiency and innovation.

The **2 AM Code** reminds us that mastering these tools isn't just about keeping pace with the digital world—it's about taking charge of your career and positioning yourself as a leader who shapes the future.

Developing Tech Skills

To thrive in today's digital economy, it's crucial to develop a range of tech skills that will elevate your career. Here are a few essential areas to explore:

- **Coding**: Learning languages like Python, JavaScript, and HTML/CSS can unlock various career opportunities, from web development to data science. Platforms like Codecademy and Udacity can get you started.

- **Data Analysis**: Tools like Excel, SQL, and Python help you interpret data and make informed decisions. Understanding data is key to strategic planning and leadership.

- **Digital Marketing**: Digital marketing skills are in high demand. Courses on SEO, social media, and content creation through platforms like HubSpot and LinkedIn Learning can sharpen your expertise.

- **Cybersecurity**: Protecting data is more critical than ever. Familiarize yourself with cybersecurity fundamentals through platforms like edX and Cybrary.

- **Project Management**: Tools like Trello, Asana, and Microsoft Project help you manage tasks efficiently and lead teams with confidence.

By developing these skills, you're not just advancing your career—you're building a foundation of knowledge that ensures long-term success and resilience in the workforce.

Empowerment Through Digital Mastery

Mastering digital skills isn't just about ticking off tasks—it's about stepping into leadership and independence. Here's how:

- **Confidence**: When you embrace digital literacy, you're no longer a passive participant—you're an architect of your success, taking the lead in your career.

- **Independence**: Digital literacy enables you to work autonomously, reducing reliance on others for technical tasks. This independence gives you control over your professional journey.

- **Leadership**: Digital expertise positions you to lead teams and drive innovation. Your skills make you a mentor to others, a voice for progress, and a champion of new technologies.

- **Resilience**: In a fast-paced job market, your ability to adapt and grow is critical. With tech skills in hand, you're prepared to navigate any challenge with confidence.

Every skill you master is a step closer to owning your expertise and commanding the respect you deserve. The 2 AM Code encourages you to embrace these opportunities, knowing that digital mastery leads to long-lasting career growth.

Online Learning Platforms

Continuous education is your tool for staying competitive, growing your expertise, and ensuring you're always moving forward. With online learning platforms, you have the flexibility to learn at your own pace while balancing your personal and professional life. Here's why it matters:

- **Stay Updated**: Industries change fast, and continuous learning keeps you ahead of new trends and technologies.

- **Career Advancement**: Gaining new skills opens the door to promotions, salary increases, and new opportunities.

- **Personal Growth**: Lifelong learning cultivates a growth mindset, empowering you to tackle challenges and grow as a leader.

With every new course, you're reinforcing your right to rise, lead, and succeed. Online platforms like Coursera, LinkedIn Learning, and edX offer courses tailored to professional women, helping you stay dynamic and empowered.

Networking and Social Media

Building a strong professional network is more than just connecting with others—it's about fostering relationships that can propel your career forward and empowering others along the way. Platforms like LinkedIn, Twitter, and Meetup are powerful tools for expanding your network, influence, and impact. Here's how to make the most of them:

- **LinkedIn**: Craft a compelling profile that highlights your skills, achievements, and professional journey. Join industry groups, engage with content, and share your own insights to increase visibility and establish yourself as a thought leader.
- **Twitter**: Participate in industry conversations, follow key leaders, and use relevant hashtags to stay informed and connect with a broader professional community. Sharing your knowledge on Twitter can also amplify your voice and contribute to important discussions.
- **Meetup**: Attend local meetups or create your own, connecting with professionals in your area to foster collaboration, growth, and innovation.

Networking in the digital age isn't just about meeting people—it's about creating opportunities, expanding your influence, and breaking barriers. And remember, networking isn't just about gaining; it's also about giving back. By sharing your knowledge and expertise with others, you pave the way for more women to rise, fostering a culture of empowerment and support.

Empowering Connections

Networking empowers you to collaborate, learn, and grow. It's a tool for creating the career and the support system you deserve:

- **Opportunities**: By connecting with industry leaders, you open doors to partnerships and projects that elevate your career.
- **Collaboration**: Networking allows you to work with others, share knowledge, and develop new skills together.
- **Support Systems**: Building strong networks connects you with mentors and peers who provide guidance and encouragement as you navigate your career.

Leverage your networks to break into male-dominated fields, gain confidence, and build relationships that foster success.

Personal Branding

Your LinkedIn profile isn't just a digital resume—it's your personal brand on a global stage, a tool to assert your authority, showcase your achievements, and attract opportunities that align with your aspirations. Your personal brand is your professional voice, and curating an online presence that reflects your expertise and leadership is key to standing out and building credibility.

Here's how to strengthen and amplify your personal brand:

- **Blogging**: Sharing your knowledge through regular blog posts positions you as a thought leader in your field, allowing your expertise to reach a wider audience.

- **Professional Website**: Your website should be more than a portfolio—it's a dynamic showcase of your work, achievements, and professional journey. Ensure it's visually appealing, easy to navigate, and reflective of your unique style and accomplishments.

- **Social Media**: Platforms like LinkedIn, Twitter, and Instagram aren't just for connecting; they are powerful tools to engage with your audience, share industry insights, and highlight your personal achievements. Use them to build connections that matter and reinforce your influence.

Your personal brand is a reflection of your impact. By consistently showcasing your skills, achievements, and thought leadership, you'll not only attract the right opportunities but also position yourself as a leader in your field, with the power to shape your professional journey on your own terms.

Remote Work Tools

The digital era has redefined how we work, offering women more control over their work-life balance. With remote work tools, you're not just managing tasks—you're designing a professional life on your own terms, with the flexibility and autonomy to succeed on your schedule. Tools like Trello, Asana, and Slack empower you to work efficiently, collaborate seamlessly, and take control of your time, ensuring that you can excel in both your personal and professional life without sacrificing one for the other.

By leveraging these tools, you create a work-life balance tailored to your needs, fueling both career and personal growth. The right tools enable you to lead teams, manage projects, and achieve your goals—no matter where you are.

Tech for Work-Life Balance

Effective time management is crucial for balancing career and personal responsibilities. Apps like Todoist, RescueTime, and Forest help you stay focused, manage tasks, and make the most of your time. Mastering these tools gives you the freedom to craft a fulfilling professional journey while maintaining a healthy work-life balance.

Mastering digital tools isn't just about proficiency—it's about transforming yourself into a leader who commands her career and shapes her future with purpose. These tools unlock limitless potential, empowering you to take control of your professional journey.

AI Essentials: Must-Have Apps for Personal and Business Growth

Mastering AI-powered apps isn't just about keeping up with technology—it's about empowering yourself to thrive, build resilience, and take control of your career. These tools support both personal growth and professional advancement, giving you the edge you need in today's digital-first world.

1. **Personal Development and Self-Efficacy**

   AI-powered coaching apps like **Replika** and **Woebot** offer mental health support and personal coaching, helping you build resilience and confidence. They provide a safe space for reflection, emotional support, and personal growth at your own pace.

2. **Professional Networking and Mentorship**

   AI-driven platforms like **LinkedIn** enhance your networking by suggesting connections, groups, and relevant content. Tools like **MentorcliQ** foster mentorships by matching you with mentors based on shared skills and goals, expanding your support system for career growth.

3. **Career Advancement and Salary Negotiation**

   With AI-powered career coaching tools like **Jobscan** and **Linke-dIn's Career Explorer**, you can receive personalized advice on resume optimization and job opportunities. **Payscale** and **Glass-door** provide salary benchmarks, empowering you to negotiate confidently and secure fair compensation.

4. **Navigating Workplace Dynamics**

   Apps like **Grammarly** and **Crystal Knows** help you refine your communication, providing real-time feedback on tone and style. **Bias detection tools** like **Textio** analyze language in job descriptions and professional documents, promoting a more inclusive workplace and ensuring your contributions are recognized for their value.

5. **Managing Work-Life Balance**

   AI personal assistants like **Google Assistant** and **Amazon Alexa** simplify your life by managing schedules and automating routine tasks, giving you more time to focus on what matters. Wellness apps like **Headspace** and **Calm** offer personalized meditation practices that help you reduce stress and maintain balance.

6. **Responding to Unwanted Advances**

   AI tools like **Botler AI** and **Callisto** offer guidance and support for women facing harassment. These platforms ensure your experiences are documented and provide legal advice on how to take action, creating safer and more supportive workplace environments.

7. **Empowering Through Knowledge**

   AI content curation apps like **Feedly** and **Pocket** keep you informed by curating relevant news, articles, and industry insights. Writing assistants like **Jasper** and **Writesonic** help you craft compelling content, from reports to blog posts, empowering you to communicate your expertise with confidence.

8. **Stress Reduction Tools**

   Stress management is essential for maintaining overall well-being. Apps like **Headspace** and **Calm** offer guided meditations, sleep aids, and relaxation practices that help you unwind, stay focused, and manage stress more effectively. Incorporating these tools into your daily routine enhances your mental health and resilience.

These AI-powered apps go beyond boosting productivity and organization—they are tools for empowerment. They equip you with the ability to master your time, make informed decisions, and face challenges with confidence. As you embrace these technologies, you'll discover that they are not just digital tools, but powerful allies, helping you thrive in every aspect of your personal and professional life.

While the personal benefits of digital tools like efficiency, stress reduction, and flexibility are transformative, their influence doesn't stop at individual growth. When women leverage these technologies to take control of their careers, the impact extends far beyond their own well-being. These advancements ripple outward, creating shifts in how economies, workplaces, and industries function on a larger scale.

The true strength of digital empowerment lies in its ability to transcend personal success. It offers the chance to bridge gender gaps, promote inclusivity, and fuel innovation globally. Let's now explore how these tools are transforming lives and communities around the world, paving the way for a more equitable and inclusive future.

Global Implications of Digital Empowerment: Transforming Lives and Communities

Digital empowerment isn't just about individual success—it's about bridging the gaps that have hindered progress for women and marginalized communities worldwide. Access to AI and digital resources provides the tools to acquire new skills, explore entrepreneurship, and connect with global networks that were previously out of reach (McKinsey & Company, 2020). Let's explore how these advancements foster inclusivity, drive economic growth, and challenge systemic barriers, ultimately paving the way for a more equitable world.

1. Bridging Gender Gaps and Creating Opportunities

Access to technology can significantly reduce gender disparities, particularly in regions where women face barriers to education and economic participation. Digital tools provide pathways for women to upskill, pursue education, and explore entrepreneurial ventures, helping to close the gender gap.

- **Skill Development and Confidence**: Platforms like Coursera and Udemy enable women to acquire qualifications that were once inaccessible, boosting their confidence and capabilities. As women gain expertise, they inspire others in their communities to follow, creating a ripple effect of empowerment.

- **Entrepreneurship and Global Reach**: Women entrepreneurs can now leverage social media and e-commerce platforms to scale their businesses, reaching customers beyond geographical limitations. This broadens opportunities for financial independence and economic participation.

2. Fostering Economic Growth Through Innovation and Entrepreneurship

Digital empowerment plays a crucial role in driving economic growth on both local and global scales. By equipping women with digital tools, they can contribute to the economy in innovative ways.

- **Job Creation**: The rise of the digital economy has led to new job opportunities in fields like digital marketing, e-commerce, software development, and data analysis. These emerging sectors create employment opportunities for women, reducing unemployment rates and increasing household incomes.

- **Promoting Innovation**: When diverse voices contribute to technological development, it leads to products and services that address real-world challenges. Women bringing their perspectives to the table can drive innovation, contributing to overall economic resilience.

3. Enhancing Global Collaboration and Communication

Digital tools have redefined how we communicate and collaborate, enabling cross-cultural and international partnerships that break down traditional barriers.

- **Global Networking**: Platforms like LinkedIn connect women with professionals across the globe, allowing them to share knowledge, seek mentorship, and collaborate on international projects. This expands their influence and builds professional networks that cross borders.

- **Cross-Cultural Collaboration**: Digital tools allow teams from diverse backgrounds to work together seamlessly, facilitating collaboration through virtual meetings, project management software, and real-time communication.

4. Addressing Systemic Barriers and Promoting Inclusivity

Technology can be a powerful tool for challenging systemic barriers that perpetuate inequality. By leveraging digital platforms, women can advocate for change, promote diversity, and amplify their voices.

- **Challenging Traditional Gender Roles**: Through online advocacy, women can challenge societal norms and stereotypes that have traditionally limited their roles. Digital platforms provide a space for women to participate in movements for gender equality and share their stories, inspiring others.

- **Promoting Diversity in Workplaces**: Digital empowerment helps organizations build inclusive workplaces by embracing remote work, flexible schedules, and diverse hiring practices. This attracts a wide range of talent and promotes creativity and innovation.

- **Raising Awareness**: Social media campaigns have the power to raise awareness about social injustices and gender inequality. By using these platforms to mobilize communities and influence policymakers, women can drive meaningful, systemic change on a larger scale.

As you embark on your journey of digital empowerment, remember the strength of the 2 AM Code: you define your career on your own terms, setting boundaries that respect your values. Technology is your ally, and each tool you use is a step toward a future where you lead with confidence, grace, and purpose.

Now, let's see how ready you are to apply these tools with the chapter assessment. This is your chance to reflect on what you've gained and take the next step in your journey toward greater empowerment.

LEVERAGING TECHNOLOGY FOR CAREER GROWTH ASSESSMENT: TECHNOLOGY UTILIZATION SCALE

Instructions: Rate each statement on a scale from 1 (Strongly disagree) to 5 (Strongly agree).

1. I use technology effectively to enhance my career.
2. I am comfortable using various digital tools and platforms.
3. I stay updated on the latest technological trends in my field.
4. I leverage social media for professional networking.
5. I use technology to improve my productivity and efficiency.
6. I can troubleshoot basic technical issues on my own.
7. I regularly learn new digital skills.
8. I use technology to collaborate with colleagues.
9. I can adapt to new technologies quickly.
10. I feel confident in my ability to use technology to achieve my career goals.

Scoring Interpretation

- 10-20: Low Utilization of Technology

Description: Individuals in this range may struggle to use technology effectively for career growth. They might feel uncomfortable with digital tools and platforms and may not stay updated on technological trends.

Action Steps:

1. Take Online Courses: Enroll in courses to improve your digital skills and learn new tools.

2. Experiment with New Technologies: Try out new digital tools and platforms relevant to your field.

3. Seek Help: Ask colleagues or mentors for guidance on using technology effectively.

- 21-35: Moderate Utilization of Technology

Description: Individuals in this range have a moderate level of comfort with technology. They use digital tools and platforms in their work but may not fully leverage them for career growth.

Action Steps:

1. Integrate Technology into Daily Routine: Use digital tools to enhance your productivity and efficiency.

2. Stay Updated: Follow industry blogs and news to stay informed about the latest technological trends.

3. Learn New Skills: Continuously seek opportunities to learn new digital skills and improve your tech proficiency.

- 36-50: High Utilization of Technology

Description: Individuals in this range are highly proficient in using technology for career growth. They stay updated on the latest trends, leverage digital tools effectively, and feel confident in their tech skills.

Action Steps:

1. Continue Leveraging Technology: Maintain your effective use of technology in your career.

2. Share Knowledge: Help colleagues improve their tech skills by sharing your knowledge and tools.

3. Reflect on Successes: Regularly reflect on how technology has enhanced your career and celebrate your achievements.

You've mastered the strategies for leveraging technology to elevate your professional presence and influence. From enhancing your digital visibility to using tools for productivity and communication, you now have a clear roadmap for thriving in today's digital world.

By completing these chapters, you've built a comprehensive skill set that empowers you to navigate the complexities of the modern workplace with confidence, authenticity, and strength. Now, take what you've learned and continue to lead with conviction, knowing you are fully equipped to thrive in both your personal and professional life.

CONCLUSION

As we close this chapter, let's hold tight to the heart of the 2 AM Code: a declaration for women to reclaim their power, especially in spaces that test our strength and resilience. In those quiet, late-night moments when doubt creeps in, remember your inner fire—an unstoppable force capable of overcoming any challenge. Together, we rise above the noise of doubt, standing firm in our truth, unapologetic in our ambition.

Empowerment is not a destination; it's a journey that demands continual growth. Each victory and setback molds us into stronger, wiser versions of ourselves. I encourage you to lean into this process—reflect deeply, seek out mentors, and build communities that lift one another higher. When we stand together, we create a legacy of resilience, strength, and hope—one that will inspire generations to come.

Now is the moment to take action. Refuse to accept the limits others have placed on you. Build connections with women who share your vision, and walk this path with courage and conviction. Reclaim your power—not just for yourself, but for all women. As you move forward, let the 2 AM Code light your way, reminding you of your strength, your voice, and your impact. The time is now—ignite your journey, inspire others, and create a ripple of change that will echo far beyond this moment. Your voice is powerful, your potential boundless—embrace it, and lead the way forward.

CHAPTER
REFLECTIVE QUESTIONS

Chapter 1: Understanding Self-Efficacy and Self-Awareness

1. What are my core strengths, and how can I leverage them more effectively in my career?

2. How do I typically respond to challenges, and what strategies can I use to strengthen my resilience in the face of setbacks?

3. In what areas of my life do I feel most confident, and how does this confidence impact my decisions and actions?

4. How often do I reflect on my thoughts and emotions, and how can I use these insights to grow my self-awareness and effectiveness?

5. What actionable steps can I take to enhance my self-efficacy and increase my belief in my ability to succeed?

The 2 AM Code: Self-efficacy is about owning your power. Reflecting on your strengths and setbacks helps you stand firm in your career without compromising your boundaries.

Chapter 2: The Power of Saying No

1. When was the last time I said no, and how did it impact my sense of control and well-being?

2. What are the key reasons I find it difficult to say no, and how can I overcome these barriers to protect my time and energy?

3. How does saying no help me prioritize my well-being and career goals, and how can I practice saying no more confidently?

4. What strategies can I use to assertively say no, without guilt, while staying true to my values?

5. How can I handle others' reactions when I say no and remain firm in maintaining my boundaries?

The 2 AM Code: Saying no is about reclaiming your space and power. It allows you to define your career and personal life on your own terms, unapologetically.

Chapter 3: Establishing and Communicating Boundaries

1. What are my personal and professional boundaries, and how can I communicate them more effectively to others?
2. How do I feel when my boundaries are respected or crossed, and what can I do to ensure they are consistently honored?
3. What are the main challenges I face in setting and maintaining boundaries, and how can I address them head-on?
4. How can I assertively communicate my boundaries, ensuring that they are clear and respected in both personal and professional settings?
5. What actions can I take to respect and honor the boundaries of others while maintaining my own?

The 2 AM Code: Setting boundaries isn't a limitation—it's an act of empowerment. Define your space and communicate your needs to protect your sense of self and dignity.

Chapter 4: Managing Inappropriate Discussions

1. How can I identify when a conversation turns inappropriate, and what signals can I look out for to recognize this early?
2. What are my strategies for confidently redirecting or shutting down inappropriate conversations, especially in professional settings?
3. How do I feel about confronting inappropriate comments, and what steps can I take to build my confidence in addressing them assertively?
4. What are the policies in my workplace regarding inappropriate discussions, and how can I ensure I am familiar with and uphold them?

5. How can I be an ally to colleagues who face inappropriate discussions, and what can I do to support them effectively?

The 2 AM Code: Your dignity is non-negotiable. By addressing inappropriate conversations, you take a stand for your values and help create a respectful environment.

Chapter 5: Understanding the Male Ego

1. How does the male ego manifest in my workplace, and how do I currently navigate these dynamics?
2. What specific strategies can I adopt to navigate and diffuse interactions that are driven by ego without diminishing my own voice or value?
3. How can I maintain my composure and assertiveness in situations where the male ego dominates the conversation?
4. What impact does the male ego have on team dynamics, and how can I lead with emotional intelligence to address it?
5. How can I provide constructive feedback to colleagues with strong egos in a way that fosters collaboration and mutual respect?

The 2 AM Code: You don't shrink yourself to accommodate egos. Instead, you lead with confidence, asserting your voice in every conversation.

Chapter 6: The Role of Eye Contact

1. How comfortable am I with maintaining eye contact, and what messages do I believe my eye contact conveys to others?
2. How can I use eye contact to demonstrate confidence and build stronger connections with colleagues and clients?
3. In what ways can I improve my eye contact skills to enhance my professional presence and influence in meetings and discussions?
4. What cultural differences should I be aware of regarding eye contact in my workplace, and how can I adjust accordingly?
5. How can I practice maintaining meaningful eye contact while staying authentic to myself?

The 2 AM Code: Eye contact is a subtle yet powerful tool. It shows that you are present, engaged, and unapologetically confident in any interaction.

Chapter 7: Understanding Appearance and Perception

1. How does my appearance influence how I'm perceived in the workplace, and what changes can I make to project more confidence and professionalism?

2. How can I express my personal style while maintaining a professional image that aligns with my career goals?

3. How do non-verbal cues, such as body language and facial expressions, complement my appearance and affect others' perceptions of me?

4. What feedback have I received about my appearance, and how can I use it to enhance my professional image without compromising my authenticity?

5. What small adjustments can I make to ensure that my appearance reflects both my personality and my professionalism?

The 2 AM Code: How you present yourself is a reflection of how you claim your space in the professional world. It's about owning your image without apology.

Chapter 8: Communication Dynamics After Hours

1. How do I feel about engaging in work-related conversations after hours, and what boundaries do I need to set to maintain balance?

2. What strategies can I use to navigate after-hours work gatherings while maintaining professionalism and personal boundaries?

3. How can I transition smoothly between professional and casual communication styles during after-hours interactions without compromising my integrity?

4. What steps can I take to ensure that my personal time is protected, even in a work culture that values after-hours communication?

5. How can I confidently handle conflicts that arise during informal, after-hours interactions?

The 2 AM Code: After-hours communication is your choice—not a demand. Set your boundaries and communicate them clearly to protect your personal time and energy.

Chapter 9: Advocating for Yourself: Salary Negotiation

1. How confident am I in discussing my salary, and what factors contribute to my level of confidence or discomfort?

2. What are my key achievements and contributions, and how do they justify a higher salary or promotion?

3. How can I better prepare for salary negotiations to ensure I approach them with confidence and clarity?

4. What strategies can I use to handle objections or counteroffers during negotiations without compromising my value?

5. If a salary increase isn't possible, how can I negotiate for other benefits that will enhance my career and well-being?

The 2 AM Code: You don't negotiate your worth—you assert it. Advocating for yourself is about claiming the compensation and respect you deserve.

Chapter 10: Building a Support Network

1. Who are the key members of my support network, and how do they contribute to my growth and success?

2. How can I strategically expand my network to include more diverse, influential, and supportive connections?

3. What value do I bring to my network, and how can I enhance that value to support mutual growth?

4. What steps can I take to stay connected with my professional network and maintain meaningful relationships over time?

5. How can I offer more mentorship and support to others within my network to help them rise alongside me?

The 2 AM Code: A strong network amplifies your power. By nurturing your connections, you build a community of growth, mentorship, and success.

Chapter 11: Leveraging Technology for Career Growth

1. How effectively am I using technology to enhance my career, and what areas of improvement should I focus on to stay competitive?

2. What new digital skills can I learn to stay ahead in my field, and how can I begin mastering them today?

3. How can I leverage social media and digital platforms more strategically for networking, learning, and professional growth?

4. What specific tools and platforms can I integrate into my daily routine to boost my productivity and efficiency?

5. How can I ensure I'm staying updated on the latest technological trends in my industry, and how can I use that knowledge to advance my career?

The 2 AM Code: Technology is your ally, not just a tool. Use it to enhance your career, define your future, and stay empowered in a digital world.

Conclusion: Turning Reflection into Empowered Action

As you work through the chapter reflective questions, know that every answer brings you closer to owning your personal and professional journey. The 2 AM Code is more than a philosophy—it's your call to action. Reflection is a powerful tool, but it's in the action that transformation truly happens.

These questions have helped you explore your strengths, confront challenges, and uncover new opportunities for growth. Now, the real work begins. Take these insights and turn them into concrete steps toward the empowered life you deserve. Each choice, every boundary set, and every decision made with intention strengthens your journey forward.

Remember, this process is continuous. Growth doesn't stop here, and neither does your impact. With every reflection, you sharpen your vision and fortify your resilience. The 2 AM Code reminds you to rise above limitations and live unapologetically on your own terms.

Now is your moment—commit to the action that will drive your empowerment, shape your career, and inspire the women who will follow in your footsteps.

REFLECT AND ACT: EMBRACING THE 2 AM CODE IN ACTION

1. Identify Patterns and Core Insights

- **Review Your Reflections**: Look closely at your answers and identify recurring themes. Where do you feel most empowered? Where do doubts still surface? The 2 AM Code asks you to embrace your power, even in your vulnerabilities.

- **Spot Key Lessons**: Highlight key realizations that reflect your inner strength. These insights reveal not just areas for improvement, but your potential for growth and resilience.

2. Set Empowering Goals and Action Plans

- **Craft 2 AM Code Goals**: Turn your reflections into empowering SMART goals (Specific, Measurable, Achievable, Relevant, Time-bound). These goals should align with your personal values and career vision. For instance, if you recognize a need to set better boundaries, set a goal to say no without guilt in both professional and personal spaces.

- **Break It Down**: Create clear, actionable steps to reach each goal. The 2 AM Code is about maintaining dignity and self-respect—each step should reflect this. If one goal is to enhance your communication skills, list actions such as practicing assertive responses or joining a public speaking group.

3. Track Your Progress with Purpose

- **Check-In Regularly**: Set time aside to reflect on your progress. Are you holding firm to your boundaries? Are you standing tall in the face of challenges? Adjust your plans as needed to stay aligned with your 2 AM Code.

- **Journal Your Empowerment Journey**: Keep a journal to track both successes and lessons. Writing down your experiences helps you recognize the progress you've made, even when it feels slow.

4. Seek Feedback, Build Support

- **Engage Mentors and Allies**: Share your reflections and goals with trusted mentors or peers who support your journey. The 2 AM Code is about collective strength—lean on those who help you grow while holding onto your dignity.

- **Foster a Supportive Community**: Join professional networks or groups of like-minded individuals where you can exchange ideas, gain feedback, and strengthen your support system.

5. Reflect, Adjust, and Evolve

- **Continuous Reflection as Power**: Reflection is a key part of the 2 AM Code. Regularly revisit your goals and assess whether you're moving in a direction that honors your values and aspirations.

- **Adapt with Grace**: Be flexible with your goals—adjust them as needed based on what you've learned. The path to empowerment is not always linear, but every adjustment is part of your growth.

6. Celebrate Every Victory, Big or Small

- **Acknowledge Your Achievements**: Every step forward is a testament to your strength and the 2 AM Code. Celebrate your wins, whether it's asserting yourself in a meeting or saying no without apology.

- **Reflect on How Far You've Come**: Take time to recognize how much you've grown. Your journey isn't just about professional success—it's about becoming the empowered, resilient leader the 2 AM Code calls you to be.

7. Apply Your Power to Real-Life Situations

- **Live the 2 AM Code**: The insights you've gained through reflection are meant to guide you in real-life situations. For example, if you've practiced handling difficult conversations, apply that assertiveness in your next meeting. Trust your inner strength to lead you.

- **Commit to Continuous Growth**: The 2 AM Code is about evolving with purpose. Use every experience as an opportunity to fine-tune your approach, learn, and rise stronger.

Conclusion: Embrace the 2 AM Code and Take Action

As you complete this reflective journey, remember that empowerment is not a one-time event—it's a continuous process. The insights you've gained here are just the beginning. Reflecting on your experiences, identifying your strengths, and acknowledging areas for growth are powerful steps, but action is what transforms knowledge into change.

By committing to the 2 AM Code, you're pledging to honor your boundaries, protect your dignity, and shape your career and life on your own terms. This is about more than personal success; it's about owning your voice, standing firm in your values, and creating a future where your potential is fully realized.

Your journey doesn't end with the last page of this book. Each goal you set, each step you take, and every moment of self-reflection is part of an ongoing commitment to growth and leadership. Stay adaptable, remain open to new opportunities, and continually adjust your path as you evolve.

Now, it's time to act. Take what you've learned, apply it with intention, and remember: your power is undeniable, your voice matters, and the time to lead is now. Let the 2 AM Code be your guide as you continue to ignite change and inspire others.

ROADMAP TO EMPOWERMENT: APPLYING THE 2:00 AM CODE

As you reach the end of this journey, it's time to take the concepts, tools, and strategies you've learned and transform them into action-able steps for long-term success. Empowerment is not a destina-tion—it's a process that requires continuous effort, reflection, and adaptation. This roadmap will guide you through each critical area we've explored in the book, helping you build a personalized plan to thrive in your career and personal life.

1. Master Self-Efficacy and Confidence

- **Set Achievable Goals:** Begin by setting small, specific goals that align with your larger ambitions. Break them into manageable steps, and celebrate each success as a building block for your self-efficacy.

  - *Action Step:* Write down three short-term and three long-term goals, focusing on areas where you want to build con-fidence.

- **Track Your Progress:** Use a journal or digital app to track your achievements. Reflect on how far you've come and the skills you've gained along the way.

  - *Action Step:* Create a monthly reflection routine to assess what you've achieved, what challenged you, and how you can continue to improve.

2. Assert Your Boundaries

- **Communicate Clearly:** Practice setting boundaries in both your personal and professional life. Be clear, concise, and firm when expressing your needs.

- □ *Action Step:* Role-play boundary-setting scenarios with a trusted colleague or friend, focusing on areas where you've struggled to assert yourself.

- **Reinforce Your Limits:** Once you've established your boundaries, be consistent in maintaining them. This will help others respect your space and time.

  - □ *Action Step:* List three situations where you need to reinforce boundaries and write out how you'll communicate them.

3. Build and Strengthen Your Network

- **Cultivate Relationships:** Connect with mentors, colleagues, and peers who can offer support, guidance, and collaboration opportunities. Networking is key to opening doors and advancing your career.

  - □ *Action Step:* Identify three key individuals in your network with whom you want to strengthen your professional relationship. Reach out to them for coffee or a virtual chat to maintain or deepen the connection.

- **Expand Your Circle:** Attend industry events, workshops, or conferences to meet new people and gain fresh perspectives.

  - □ *Action Step:* Commit to attending at least one professional event or networking session each quarter.

4. Master the Art of Negotiation

- **Prepare for Salary Negotiations:** Know your worth and gather data to support your value when entering salary or promotion discussions. Practice negotiating with confidence and clarity.

  - □ *Action Step:* Research industry salary standards and prepare a list of your achievements to bring to your next performance review.

- **Negotiate Beyond Salary:** Negotiate for growth opportunities, flexible work arrangements, or resources that will enhance your professional development.

□ *Action Step:* Identify one non-monetary benefit you'd like to negotiate in your current role and outline how it would benefit both you and your employer.

5. Leverage Technology for Career Advancement

- **Stay Tech-Savvy:** Continuously update your digital skills by learning new technologies, apps, and tools that can enhance your productivity and career growth.

  □ *Action Step:* Set a goal to learn one new technology or digital tool every quarter that is relevant to your field.

- **Use Digital Empowerment Tools:** Implement AI-driven solutions, productivity apps, or online learning platforms to boost your efficiency and knowledge.

  □ *Action Step:* Subscribe to one professional development platform (e.g., LinkedIn Learning, Coursera) and complete a relevant course to strengthen a specific skill.

6. Embrace Cultural Sensitivity and Inclusion

- **Be Mindful of Diversity:** Recognize and appreciate cultural differences in professional settings. Make inclusion a priority in your interactions and workplace decisions.

  □ *Action Step:* Practice empathy by learning about the cultural backgrounds of your colleagues and considering their perspectives in group settings.

- **Champion Inclusivity:** Be a voice for inclusive practices within your organization. Advocate for policies that support diversity, equity, and inclusion.

  □ *Action Step:* Join or support an inclusion initiative at work or in your industry that promotes diversity and equality.

7. Maintain Your Work-Life Balance

- **Set Boundaries Between Work and Personal Time:** Avoid burnout by creating clear separations between your work and home life. Prioritize rest, leisure, and personal development.

- *Action Step:* Create a daily routine that includes dedicated time for relaxation, self-care, and activities you enjoy outside of work.

- **Practice Mindfulness:** Incorporate mindfulness and stress-management techniques to stay grounded and maintain mental clarity.

  - *Action Step:* Start a mindfulness practice—whether through meditation, journaling, or regular exercise—to improve focus and resilience.

8. Reflect, Reassess, and Adapt

- **Evaluate Your Progress Regularly:** Empowerment is an evolving process. Take time to assess where you are, what you've achieved, and where you want to go next.

  - *Action Step:* Schedule quarterly check-ins with yourself to review your progress using this roadmap. Reflect on what's working, where you've faced challenges, and how you can adapt moving forward.

- **Stay Flexible:** Be open to change and growth. As new opportunities arise, adjust your goals and strategies to continue thriving in your personal and professional journey.

  - *Action Step:* Set a flexible goal each year to explore a new direction or passion in your career, ensuring you stay adaptable and engaged.

Final Empowerment Challenge:

To truly embody *The 2:00 AM Code*, challenge yourself to take one bold action in the next 30 days that will advance your career or personal growth. Whether it's applying for a leadership role, setting a difficult boundary, or starting a new learning journey, this final step will cement your commitment to continuous empowerment.

THE 2 AM CODE: YOUR POWER PATHWAY (PLEDGE)

Objective: Transform the insights and principles of the 2 AM Code into a personalized empowerment roadmap, guiding you through your career and personal life with confidence and purpose.

Step 1: Define Your "2 AM Moment"

Think back to a time when you felt challenged, pressured, or doubted—when you were on the verge of compromising your values or career choices. Maybe it was a moment where you said "yes" when you truly wanted to say "no," or when you felt disempowered in a situation.

Now, take a deep breath and reflect. What did that moment teach you? How could you have responded differently, embracing the principles of the 2 AM Code? Write a brief reflection on how you can reframe that moment with the wisdom you have now.

This step brings awareness to past experiences, helping you rewrite those moments through the empowering lens of the 2 AM Code. Your awareness is the first step in reclaiming your power.

Step 2: Set Your Empowerment Goals

Let's now turn reflection into action. Divide your empowerment map into four core areas, representing the pillars of your empowered life:

Career Goals: Where do you want to be professionally in the next 6 months? What actions can you take to make that vision a reality? Be bold—this is your moment to dream, plan, and take control.

Boundary Setting: Identify two areas in your life—one personal, one professional—where you need to set or reinforce boundaries.

What words will you use to communicate these boundaries assertively, embodying your inner strength?

Personal Growth: What skill or mindset shift will help you step into your fullest potential? Think about one area where you can expand and grow, and create a plan to start building that skill or habit today.

Network and Support: Who are the people that uplift and empower you? List your mentors, colleagues, and supporters. How will you strengthen these connections and use your network to fuel your journey?

These goals are your roadmap to living the 2 AM Code. Each one is a commitment to your own growth, ensuring that every step forward aligns with your values.

Step 3: Map Your Empowerment Actions

Now, let's get practical. For each of your goals from Step 2, identify two or three specific, concrete actions you will take in the next 30 days. Make these actions intentional, realistic, and empowering.

For example: "In the next 30 days, I will update my LinkedIn profile, join a networking group, and practice saying no to one task that overwhelms me."

These actions are your commitment to living the 2 AM Code in everyday life. They move you from reflection to execution, helping you take empowered action with clarity and purpose.

Step 4: Visualize Your Success

On the final page of your empowerment map, take a moment to visualize what success looks and feels like for you. Close your eyes and imagine yourself fully embodying the 2 AM Code.

Write Your Vision Statement: "In six months, I see myself…"

Describe how you've grown, how you've set and respected boundaries, and how new opportunities have unfolded as a result of your empowered choices. This vision is your guiding light, a powerful reminder of where you're headed and how capable you are of getting there.

Step 5: Your 2 AM Power Pledge

Now it's time to take the final, most empowering step—making your 2 AM Commitment. This is more than just a pledge; it's your personal declaration to live by the 2 AM Code, a vow to honor your values, set unshakable boundaries, and lead your life with confidence and strength.

Your Power Pledge: Write your pledge in your own words, something that resonates deeply with who you are and the empowered path you are ready to embrace. Here's an example to guide you:

"I pledge to embody the 2 AM Code in every aspect of my life. I will prioritize my values, set clear and firm boundaries, and own my journey with unwavering confidence, strength, and grace. My career, my choices, my power—on my terms, without compromise or hesitation. I stand firm in my worth, and I commit to rising, leading, and thriving with dignity and courage."

Once you've written your personal commitment, **sign and date** it. This is your contract with yourself, a powerful promise to carry the principles of the 2 AM Code forward, no matter what challenges lie ahead.

This is the moment where your empowerment journey truly begins. Every time you feel tested, every time doubt tries to creep in, return to this pledge. Let it remind you of your strength, your values, and your unwavering commitment to living the life you deserve—on your own terms.

Sign it, own it, live it. Your empowered future starts now.

OWN YOUR POWER: THE 2 AM CODE COMMITMENT (CONTRACT)

By signing this contract, I commit to embracing my personal power, standing firm in my values, and pursuing my career and life with confidence, dignity, and purpose. These are the principles I vow to live by:

1. I Own My Power (Self-Efficacy and Self-Awareness)

- I pledge to recognize my strengths, reflect on my challenges, and stand firm in my self-worth. I will not compromise my boundaries to fit into spaces where I deserve to thrive.

2. I Reclaim My Space (The Power of Saying No)

- I commit to saying no unapologetically when my time, energy, or values are at stake. I will define my career and personal life on my terms, not others'.

3. I Set Boundaries (Establishing and Communicating Boundaries)

- I will establish and communicate my boundaries clearly. My boundaries are not a limitation but an act of self-respect and empowerment, protecting my sense of self and dignity.

4. I Stand for Respect (Managing Inappropriate Discussions)

- ▫ I will not tolerate disrespect or inappropriate behavior. I commit to addressing uncomfortable situations, standing up for my values, and fostering respectful environments.

5. I Lead with Confidence (Understanding the Male Ego)

- ▫ I will not shrink myself to accommodate the ego of others. I will assert my voice in every conversation and lead with confidence, regardless of who's at the table.

6. I Engage with Presence (The Role of Eye Contact)

- ▫ I will use eye contact as a powerful tool to show my confidence, presence, and engagement. I am not afraid to be seen or heard in any room.

7. I Present Myself Authentically (Understanding Appearance and Perception)

- ▫ I pledge to own my professional image and how I show up in the world. I will express my personal style while maintaining a sense of self-assurance and professionalism.

8. I Control My Time (Communication Dynamics After Hours)

- ▫ I commit to setting boundaries around after-hours communication. I will protect my personal time and energy, engaging on my terms, not out of obligation.

9. I Assert My Worth (Advocating for Yourself: Salary Negotiation)

- ▫ I will advocate for myself unapologetically in salary and benefit negotiations. I know my worth, and I will not settle for less than what I deserve.

10. I Build My Support Network (Building a Support Network)

- □ I commit to cultivating a network of like-minded professionals who uplift and empower me. I will give back to my network and contribute to a community of shared success.

11. I Harness Technology as My Ally (Leveraging Technology for Career Growth)

- □ I pledge to embrace technology as a tool of empowerment, using it to further my career, enhance my productivity, and stay on the cutting edge of my industry.

My Empowerment Declaration:

I choose to live by **The 2 AM Code**, honoring myself, my values, and my ambitions. With each commitment, I step into my power, create opportunities, and lead with confidence. I will embrace my full potential and use it to inspire others.

Signed: _____

Date:_____

AUTHOR BIO FOR "THE EMPOWERMENT PLAYBOOK: THE 2:00 AM CODE FOR CAREER AND PERSONAL SUCCESS"

Lisa Anugwom Narh is a dynamic professional with a career spanning over a decade in leadership, compliance, and human resource management across various industries. With a Master of Science in Management and Leadership from Pepperdine University and a passion for fostering inclusive, equitable workplaces, Lisa has consistently demonstrated excellence in roles that require emotional intelligence, strategic decision-making, and the ability to drive organizational change.

Born in America to Nigerian parents, Lisa was raised in a home deeply rooted in traditional and cultural values. Her upbringing in a two-parent household, with parents who have been married for 44 years, instilled in her the importance of family, integrity, and perseverance. These values have shaped not only her personal life but also her professional journey. Lisa's background has given her a unique perspective on balancing cultural expectations with modern career challenges, making her uniquely qualified to guide women in their pursuit of career and personal success.

In her career, Lisa has held key roles such as Global Account Manager, Human Resources Manager, and Equal Employment Opportunity Compliance Officer, where she has been responsible for ensuring fairness, compliance, and the empowerment of diverse workforces. Currently, she serves with Los Angeles County, overseeing multimillion-dollar contracts while fostering an environment where equity and growth thrive. Her ability to mentor, guide, and support professionals through complex workplace dynamics makes her the perfect voice for empowering women in the workplace.

Lisa's personal life is just as rich and fulfilling. She has been married to her husband, Winfred, since November 11, 2011, and together they are raising two daughters, Bliss and Icelyn, who have both consistently been on the principal's honor roll throughout their academic journeys. With emotional intelligence as her greatest strength, Lisa brings the same compassion, wisdom, and assertiveness to her family that she encourages in the women she empowers through her work and writing.

In "The Empowerment Playbook: The 2:00 AM Code for Career and Personal Success," Lisa draws on her vast professional experience, her cultural heritage, and her personal journey to create a compelling guide for women striving to succeed in their careers without compromising their values or dignity. Her blend of personal insights and practical strategies makes this book a powerful tool for any woman ready to embrace her potential, set boundaries, and live life on her own terms.

REFERENCES

Chapter 1

1. Bandura, A. (1997). *Self-efficacy: The exercise of control.* W.H. Freeman.

2. Duval, S., & Wicklund, R. A. (1972). *A theory of objective self-awareness.* Academic Press.

3. Kabat-Zinn, J. (2012). *Mindfulness for beginners: Reclaiming the present moment—and your life.* Sounds True.

Chapter 2

1. Goleman, D. (1995). *Emotional intelligence: Why it can matter more than IQ.* Bantam Books.

2. Hofstede, G. (1980). *Culture's consequences: International differences in work-related values.* SAGE Publications.

3. O'Neill, O. A., & O'Reilly, C. A. (2011). Reducing the backlash effect: Self-monitoring and women's promotions. *Journal of Occupational and Organizational Psychology, 84*(4), 825-846.

4. Rudman, L. A. (1998). Self-promotion as a risk factor for women: The costs and benefits of counterstereotypical impression management. *Journal of Personality and Social Psychology, 74*(3), 629.

5. Salter, A. (1949). *Conditioned reflex therapy: The application of Pavlovian theory to the treatment of neurosis.* Farrar, Straus and Giroux.

6. Wolpe, J. (1958). *Psychotherapy by reciprocal inhibition.* Stanford University Press.

Chapter 3

1. Ashforth, B. E., Kreiner, G. E., & Fugate, M. (2000). All in a day's work: Boundaries and micro role transitions. *Academy of Management Review, 25*(3), 472-491.

2. Cloud, H., & Townsend, J. (1992). *Boundaries: When to say yes, how to say no to take control of your life.* Zondervan.

3. Fisher, R., & Ury, W. (1981). *Getting to yes: Negotiating agreement without giving in.* Penguin Books.

4. Goleman, D. (1995). *Emotional intelligence: Why it can matter more than IQ.* Bantam Books.

5. Hofstede, G. (1980). *Culture's consequences: International differences in work-related values.* SAGE Publications.

6. Markman, H. J., Stanley, S. M., & Blumberg, S. L. (1994). *Fighting for your marriage.* Jossey-Bass.

7. Peterson, J. B. (1999). *Maps of meaning: The architecture of belief.* Routledge.

Chapter 4

1. Fisher, R., & Ury, W. (1981). *Getting to yes: Negotiating agreement without giving in.* Penguin Books.

2. Goffman, E. (1967). *Interaction ritual: Essays on face-to-face behavior.* Doubleday Anchor.

3. Goleman, D. (1995). *Emotional intelligence: Why it can matter more than IQ.* Bantam Books.

4. Graves, R. (1955). *The Greek myths.* Penguin Books.

5. Homer. (1980). *The Iliad.* Penguin Classics.

6. Jablin, F. M. (1987). *Handbook of organizational communication: An interdisciplinary perspective.* SAGE Publications.

7. Mintzberg, H. (1973). *The nature of managerial work.* Harper & Row.

8. Nilsen, D. (1993). *Humor in business communication: A study of humor in managerial settings.* Cengage.

9. Peterson, J. B. (1999). *Maps of meaning: The architecture of belief.* Routledge.

10. Scharff, S., & Broidy, L. (1997). *Collaborative communication in the workplace.* SAGE Publications.

Chapter 5

1. Carnegie, D. (1936). *How to win friends and influence people.* Simon & Schuster.

2. Connell, R. W. (2005). *Masculinities.* University of California Press.

3. Covey, S. R. (1989). *The 7 habits of highly effective people: Powerful lessons in personal change.* Free Press.

4. Eagly, A. H., & Carli, L. L. (2007). *Through the labyrinth: The truth about how women become leaders.* Harvard Business Review Press.

5. Goffman, E. (1959). *The presentation of self in everyday life.* Doubleday Anchor.

6. Goleman, D. (1995). *Emotional intelligence: Why it can matter more than IQ.* Bantam Books.

7. Hogan, R., & Kaiser, R. B. (2005). *What we know about leadership.* Review of General Psychology.

8. Horney, K. (1937). *The neurotic personality of our time.* Norton & Co.

9. Kanter, R. M. (1977). *Men and women of the corporation.* Basic Books.

10. Kimmel, M. (1996). *Manhood in America: A cultural history.* The Free Press.

11. Rudman, L. A. (1998). Self-promotion as a risk factor for women: The costs and benefits of counterstereotypical impression management. *Journal of Personality and Social Psychology, 74*(3), 629–645.

12. Scharff, S., & Broidy, L. (1997). *Collaborative communication in the workplace.* SAGE Publications.

13. Tannen, D. (1990). *You just don't understand: Women and men in conversation.* Ballantine Books.

Chapter 6:

1. Aristotle. *Rhetoric*. Translated by W. Rhys Roberts, Oxford University Press.

2. Argyle, M. (1972). *The psychology of interpersonal behaviour*. Penguin Books.

3. Brennan, M. (2007). *Speech and thought presentation in written and spoken English*. Palgrave Macmillan.

4. Burgoon, J. K., Buller, D. B., & Woodall, W. G. (1996). *Nonverbal communication: The unspoken dialogue*. McGraw-Hill.

5. Ekman, P., & Friesen, W. V. (1969). *The repertoire of nonverbal behavior: Categories, origins, usage, and coding*. Semiotica.

6. Givens, D. B. (2005). *The nonverbal dictionary of gestures, signs & body language cues*. Spokane, WA: Center for Nonverbal Studies.

7. Goleman, D. (1995). *Emotional intelligence: Why it can matter more than IQ*. Bantam Books.

8. Hall, E. T. (1966). *The hidden dimension*. Doubleday.

9. Hartenstein, J. (2002). *The art of reading faces: A guide to understanding the human face*. Simon & Schuster.

10. Kleinke, C. L. (1986). Gaze and eye contact: A research review. *Psychological Bulletin, 100*(1), 78–100.

11. Knapp, M. L., & Hall, J. A. (2009). *Nonverbal communication in human interaction* (6th ed.). Wadsworth Publishing.

12. Mehrabian, A. (1981). *Silent messages: Implicit communication of emotions and attitudes* (2nd ed.). Wadsworth Publishing.

13. Pease, A., & Pease, B. (2004). *The definitive book of body language*. Bantam Books.

14. Philpot, R. T. (2001). *Nonverbal communication in professional settings*. Pearson.

15. Tomasello, M. (2008). *Origins of human communication*. MIT Press.

Chapter 7

1. Crane, D. (2012). *Fashion and its social agendas: Class, gender, and identity in clothing*. University of Chicago Press.

2. Damhorst, M. L. (1990). In search of a common thread: Classification of information communicated through dress. *Clothing and Textiles Research Journal, 8*(2), 1-12.

3. Dion, K., Berscheid, E., & Walster, E. (1972). What is beautiful is good. *Journal of Personality and Social Psychology, 24*(3), 285–290.

4. Dittmar, H. (1992). *The social psychology of material possessions: To have is to be*. Harvester Wheatsheaf.

5. Dittmar, H. (2007). *Consumer culture, identity, and well-being: The search for the "good life" and the "body perfect"*. Psychology Press.

6. Entwistle, J. (2000). *The fashioned body: Fashion, dress and modern social theory*. Polity Press.

7. Entwistle, J. (2015). *Fashioning models: Image, text and industry*. Bloomsbury Publishing.

8. Goffman, E. (1959). *The presentation of self in everyday life*. Doubleday Anchor Books.

9. Hall, E. T. (1966). *The hidden dimension*. Doubleday.

10. Knapp, M. L., & Hall, J. A. (2009). *Nonverbal communication in human interaction* (6th ed.). Wadsworth Publishing.

11. Rafaeli, A., & Pratt, M. G. (1993). Tailored meanings: On the meaning and impact of dress in organizations. *Academy of Management Review, 18*(1), 32-55.

12. Simmel, G. (1957). Fashion. *The American Journal of Sociology, 62*(6), 541-558.

13. Todorov, A., Said, C. P., & Verosky, S. C. (2005). The contribution of face perception to social impression formation. *Social Cognitive and Affective Neuroscience, 1*(1), 18–25.

Chapter 8:

1. Derks, D., van Duin, D., Tims, M., & Bakker, A. B. (2014). Smartphone use and work-home interference: The moderating role of social norms and employee work engagement. *Journal of Occupational and Organizational Psychology, 88*(1), 155-177.

2. Fleming, P. (2015). *The myth of work-life balance: The challenge of our time for men, women, and societies*. Palgrave Macmillan.

3. Goffman, E. (1959). *The presentation of self in everyday life*. Doubleday Anchor Books.

4. Greenbaum, J. (2019). *How to create a work-life balance culture in your workplace*. New York: HR Press.

5. Mazmanian, M., Orlikowski, W. J., & Yates, J. (2013). The autonomy paradox: The implications of mobile email devices for knowledge professionals. *Organization Science, 24*(5), 1337-1357.

6. Schneider, S. M. (2016). Addressing the unique challenges of healthcare administration. *Healthcare Management Review, 41*(3), 1-12.

7. Turel, O., Serenko, A., & Bontis, N. (2011). Family and work-related consequences of addiction to organizational pervasive technologies. *Information & Management, 48*(2-3), 88-95.

Chapter 9:

1. Babcock, L., & Laschever, S. (2003). *Women Don't Ask: Negotiation and the Gender Divide*. Princeton University Press.

2. Bass, B. M. (1985). *Leadership and Performance Beyond Expectations*. Free Press.

3. Edelman, L. B., Erlanger, H. S., & Lande, J. (1993). Internal Dispute Resolution: The Transformation of Civil Rights in the Workplace. *Law and Society Review, 27*(3), 497-534.

4. Fisher, R., & Ury, W. (1981). *Getting to Yes: Negotiating Agreement Without Giving In*. Penguin Books.

5. Guerin, L. (2014). *The Essential Guide to Handling Workplace Harassment & Discrimination*. Nolo.

6. Gutman, A. M. (2017). *Sexual Harassment and Workplace Discrimination: Legal Standards and Social Responses*. Oxford University Press.

7. Hersey, P., & Blanchard, K. H. (1969). Life Cycle Theory of Leadership. *Training and Development Journal, 23*(5), 26-34.

8. Kolb, D. M. (2016). *Negotiating at Work: Turn Small Wins into Big Gains*. Jossey-Bass.

9. Shell, G. R. (2006). *Bargaining for Advantage: Negotiation Strategies for Reasonable People*. Penguin Books.

10. Yukl, G. (2013). *Leadership in Organizations* (8th ed.). Pearson.

Chapter 10:

1. Baker, W. (2000). *Achieving Success through Social Capital: Tapping the Hidden Resources in Your Personal and Business Networks.* Jossey-Bass.

2. Briggs, C. (2016). *Networking for People Who Hate Networking: A Field Guide for Introverts, the Overwhelmed, and the Underconnected.* Berrett-Koehler Publishers.

3. Brown, B. (2013). *Daring Greatly: How the Courage to Be Vulnerable Transforms the Way We Live, Love, Parent, and Lead.* Penguin Random House.

4. Cross, R., & Thomas, R. J. (2008). *The Network Secrets of Great Change Agents.* Harvard Business Review.

5. Eagly, A. H., & Carli, L. L. (2007). *Through the Labyrinth: The Truth About How Women Become Leaders.* Harvard Business Press.

6. Edmondson, A. C. (1999). Psychological Safety and Learning Behavior in Work Teams. *Administrative Science Quarterly, 44*(2), 350-383.

7. Edmondson, A. C. (2019). *The Fearless Organization: Creating Psychological Safety in the Workplace for Learning, Innovation, and Growth.* John Wiley & Sons.

8. Ely, R. J., Ibarra, H., & Kolb, D. M. (2011). Taking Gender into Account: Theory and Design for Women's Leadership Development Programs. *Academy of Management Learning & Education, 10*(3), 474-493.

9. Ellis, J. J. (1996). *Founding Brothers: The Revolutionary Generation.* Alfred A. Knopf.

10. Goffee, R., & Jones, G. (2006). *Why Should Anyone Be Led by You?: What It Takes to Be an Authentic Leader.* Harvard Business Review Press.

11. Granovetter, M. S. (1973). The Strength of Weak Ties. *American Journal of Sociology,

Chapter 11:

1. Batra, G., et al. (2020). *Artificial Intelligence for Women's Empowerment: Opportunities and Risks.* UN Women.

2. Codagnone, C., et al. (2018). *Digital Skills in the EU Labor Market*. European Commission.

3. Kumar, V., et al. (2019). *Artificial Intelligence in Business: A Roadmap for Adoption*. MIT Sloan Management Review.

4. McKinsey & Company. (2020). *The Power of Parity: Advancing Women's Equality in the Workplace*.

5. PWC. (2018). *Women in Tech: Time to Close the Gender Gap*.

6. Russell, S., & Norvig, P. (2020). *Artificial Intelligence: A Modern Approach*. Pearson.

7. Sunstein, C. R. (2019). *Algorithms, Bias, and Fairness*. American Economic Review.

8. West, D. M. (2018). *The Future of Work: Robots, AI, and Automation*. Brookings Institution Press.

www.ingramcontent.com/pod-product-compliance
Lightning Source LLC
Chambersburg PA
CBHW041626140626
46547CB00030B/1091